More Than a Play of Fancy

More Than a Play of Fancy

More Than a Play of Fancy

Spirit in the Works of William Shakespeare

Willem Frederik Veltman

Translated by Philip Mees

SteinerBooks | 2015

SteinerBooks | Anthroposophic Press
610 Main Street
Great Barrington, Massachusetts 01230
www.steinerbooks.org

Originally published as *Meer dan Een spel van de verbeelding: Geestelijke realiteiten in het wek van Shakespeare* by Uitgeverij Vrij Geestesleven (now Uitgeverij Christofoor); Zeist, Netherlands, 1989.

Translated from the Dutch by Philip Mees.

Library of Congress Control Number: 2015948090

Print ISBN: 978-1-62148-141-6
eBook ISBN: 978-1-62148-142-3

Printed in the USA

The Shakespeare quotations were taken from *The Complete Works of William Shakespeare*, Hamlyn Publishing Group Limited, 13th Impression 1970. References to act and scene after a quotation are given as (1.2): Act 1, scene 2.

Contents

FOREWORD

More than a play of fancy

The views I present in this book, and which I have tried to put into practice for many years in my work as a stage director, have never paled. On the contrary, they have only become more distinct. In theater, the point is not to try and show realistic or psychological truth, but to incorporate realism and psychology into a kind of higher imagination. I call *imagination* the force that is "more than a play of fancy." It brings to expression a reality of a spiritual character—not symbolism or allegory, but spiritual images such as we meet in myths, sagas, and fairy tales.

Inspired by Rudolf Steiner's Spiritual Science I discovered that many dramatic pictures in Shakespeare's works are filled with a higher, imaginative reality. The title of this book is inspired by Hippolyta's words in *A Midsummer Night's Dream* when she explains to Theseus that "the dream of the midsummer night" is no "fancy"; it is more than that, it is a higher truth.

I am convinced that for today's audience it is necessary to modernize Shakespeare's work in a certain sense, but I understand this in a different way from most currently prevailing views. As I see it, modernization could mean searching for the imaginative level in Shakespeare's work and making this visible and audible by purely artistic means: diction, gesture, movement, staging, sets, costumes, and lighting.

These essays about a few of Shakespeare's most beautiful and famous comedies and tragedies should not be viewed as invented, theoretical interpretations. I have put these plays on the stage with 17 and 18-year-olds, but I have also put my thoughts and feelings deeply into them, have gone into them with my whole being. In that effort, scene after scene gradually became transparent, and higher realities manifested themselves to me. I have put nothing into these essays that did not speak of its own accord from the dramatic scenes and poetic language of Shakespeare himself.

Wherever I have described cultural-historic and spiritual-scientific facts and insights I have done so only to clarify the imaginations that speak for themselves.

This book is also a witness: it wants to be a witness to the durability and indestructibility of the spirit at a time which is in many ways hostile to all spirit. Among the mighty light beacons of humanity I count William Shakespeare as one of the great trailblazers of a new era in which human consciousness will again be open to spiritual reality in the form of images.

Willem F. Veltman

I

THE MERCHANT OF VENICE

———

The Mystery of Music

The inscription on the leaden casket

Goethe once gave a deeply personal testimony of Shakespeare in a conversation with his young friend Eckermann, who diligently preserved these words that radiate like stars into the culture of Europe: "Shakespeare … who is certainly a higher kind of being to whom I look up and whom I venerate."

Goethe was right. What did he perceive in Shakespeare that led him to this confession? Was it his poetic and dramatic mastery, his psychological depth and fullness, his humanity? Yes, but he found more in Shakespeare than these great qualities which he also recognized and respected in other poets. In another conversation, in which Dante is mentioned, the sharply listening Eckermann noticed that Goethe, in lieu of the word "talent" used the word "nature." This word "nature," with the connotation of a poet's genius, is, in the sense in which Goethe used it, also applicable to Shakespeare. It indicates the recognition of an extraordinary spiritual power; he also saw this power in Raphael and Mozart.

Shakespeare's creative genius drew from the all-encompassing depths of the spiritual world. In modern times, the realism and psychological characterizations in his dramatic works have been especially admired. He

1

was the model for the dramatic arts of the romantics; Goethe, the prince of German classicism, venerated him as a being of a higher order.

Our generation will do justice to Shakespeare only if our admiration and insight penetrate to the spiritual sources from which his creations arose—when we discover the wondrous power of inspiration that made him not only the great master teacher of Goethe, the epitome of Romanticism, but also the undisputed giant of modern theater. This study wants to make a contribution to the discovery of these sources, to the encounter with that spiritual force that is today more recognized and can be more immediately experienced than ever before.

Why is virtually every learned commentary on Shakespeare's dramas inadequate? Why is it that penetrating analyses, profound treatises, historical, philosophical or psychological approaches, despite the interest and respect they show for the works, are often so unsatisfying?

No doubt this is because the Shakespeare drama, in its essential character, is not susceptible to any intellectual approach. His work is in no way realistic in the sense of Ibsen or other modern playwrights. What we call realism in Shakespeare—his roughness, his full-blooded human authenticity—is more akin to the dream than to the pale-grey waking consciousness of the nineteenth century. Dreams nourished out of the reality of the spiritual world—that is what these powerful soul scenes are. These are not shadows in the night such as our usual dreams are, but brightly colored, vehemently moving myths, woven from the dynamic substance of a world of ideas that awakens the enchanted spectator to a higher consciousness without taking him away from the earth.

There are many ways in which the soul can enter into

this work. It may surrender to it as to an immediate sensation. In enjoyment and admiration, seized by fear and awe, swept along in the stream of dramatic action, the spectator or reader lives in an elementary emotion that develops like a sensory occurrence.

Things change when the analyzing intellect sets itself over against this enchanted world. It tries to explain, to criticize; it runs up against contradictions, looks for influences; it argues to the point where the creator of all this is shriveled up to a clever little actor in whose name some unknown genius published his works. When this intellect belongs to an illustrious soul named Voltaire, it finishes the phenomenon of Shakespeare off in a few short strokes: a drunken wild man. In this specific case, the intellectual judgment may have been colored by the jealousy of a third-rate dramatist in the presence of a grand master. A scientific approach to a work of art is often respectable but not to the point, because art reflects reality in much broader circles of resonance than those of intellectual thinking.

Is there then, besides the elementary and analytical approaches, no other, more real way to enter into Shakespeare? The subject of this contemplation, *The Merchant of Venice*, gives us a fruitful indication by its imagery. The Venetian Bassanio can conquer the Lady of Belmont only if he makes the right choice of three little caskets, one of which contains her picture. This little casket has the following inscription: "Who chooseth me must give and hazard all he hath." The key to Portia's *image* also means obtaining her real person. The motto of the correct casket asks for total surrender. Bassanio's true love for Portia leads him to the right choice, but he does not act impulsively out of elementary feelings. He considers, just like his predecessors Morocco and Arragon. His intellectual thoughtfulness, however, is carried on the wings of his love; music sounds while he thinks. This enables him to see through the outer appearance. Morocco and Arragon could not do this. The fruits of their considerations are death and folly. Bassanio harvests the golden fruit of reality.

The theme of the three little caskets in *The Merchant of Venice* is an exact parable for an approach that touches on spiritual sources I mentioned before. Mythological images—and that is what all Shakespeare's dream realities are—can be known without losing their luster through human thinking when thinking has been transformed into a cognitive force by love. This kind of thinking is akin to a concentrated surrender in the meditation: "it must give and hazard all it hath." I was brought to this in my work with Shakespeare's plays because I had to direct students 17 and 18-year-olds on the stage, students for whom it was my first and foremost intention to make the spiritual reality of this work fruitful for their education.

Explanations of mythological images are susceptible to the same dangers that threatened the suitors of Portia: death and folly hide here also in little gold and silver caskets. However, the dramatic situations which I am calling here "myths" and "dream realities" have, at the same time, such deep roots in life in Shakespeare's environment, that pure speculation is exposed as false more quickly than in the usual dissertations on mythology. Therefore, with Morocco and Arragon as clear warning signs, let us proceed and contemplate one of the most delicious poetical creations in the world in the light of Goethe's testimony: as a revelation from a world of a higher order to which our time is longing for access.

The story of the Merchant

Shakespeare's work has nothing to do with symbolism or

allegory. A symbol is a sign, a glyph, a seemingly primitive indication of a spiritual reality that does not itself appear, but the symbol is pregnant with it. The spiritual potential gives the symbol a magical effect that can be used either for good or for evil. Symbols arise mostly when the human being is not free, as in ancient Egypt, when human society could still be likened to a community of bees. Symbolism is not yet true art. It appears in early, archaic stages of the development of a culture. Allegory stands at the opposite pole; it is no longer art, it is a mere abstract play of shadows. In between the two stands true art, daughter of freedom. Creative fantasy forms images in which spiritual reality makes its appearance. The substance that art uses, understood in its broadest sense, is derived from the sense world, but it is molded in such a way that the spiritual potential shines out through it.

Myths and fairy tales are not the result of fantasy. Their imagery, however, is very closely related to the products of creative fantasy, because the power of fantasy is a living remnant of an old stage of human consciousness that gave birth to fairy tales and mythology. In Shakespeare the images of fantasy are so intense, the spiritual charge is so strong, that he reaches up again to mythological consciousness. But it is not a reaching back, although his work often makes use of Greek mythology, something which cannot be explained only out of the spirit of the Renaissance that was living in his time. It is a new attainment which brings future forces with it. *The Merchant of Venice* reveals this mythological picture element to a high degree.

Although the setting and the story of this play, like those of most of Shakespeare's dramas, are derived from older or contemporary examples, it is his genius that brings out this picture quality with so much power.

Let us now trace the development of these dramatic pictures.

Antonio, a wealthy Venetian merchant, feels depressed, and he does not understand why. His bosom friend Bassanio speaks with him about his love for the fair Portia, Lady of Belmont, for whose hand he would like to sue if he but had the means to do so in a worthy manner. Antonio puts his fortune at Bassanio's disposal, but because his merchant vessels are all at sea he has no ready cash. However, he is willing to guarantee a large sum that will be borrowed from Shylock, a Jewish usurer. Shylock hates Antonio because the latter abuses him and even more because Antonio lends money without interest, thus putting the usurers at a disadvantage. The loan is made; Antonio obligates himself to repay the sum of three thousand ducats in three months. Should he not live up to the agreement, Shylock has the right to a pound of flesh from Antonio's body.

In Belmont, where Portia rules, many suitors come to woo the fair and rich heiress. She is not free in her choice, nor in her refusal, because in his last will her father has stated that the man who may call Portia his own must make the correct choice from three little caskets, one of gold, one of silver and one of lead. The Prince of Morocco tries his luck. He chooses the golden casket which contains a skull. He loses and departs.

In the meantime we have seen how in Venice the merry servant of Shylock, Launcelot, walks out on his master to the distress of Shylock's sweet daughter Jessica. But Jessica herself is concocting a plan to elope with her lover Lorenzo, a friend of Bassanio. During the night, while Shylock is away from home, Jessica is abducted by her lover.

That same night Bassanio and his friend Gratiano leave for Belmont. In Portia's realm the Prince of Arragon makes his appearance. He also makes a wrong choice: he chooses the silver casket which contains a clown's head.

In Venice very bad news is received of Antonio's ships. Shylock is desperate about the loss of his daughter, but most of all about the money and the valuables she has taken with her on her flight. His only consolation is Antonio's misfortune.

Bassanio is received in Belmont; he wins the bride by choosing the leaden casket. His friend, the happy Gratiano, without much ado conquers the heart of Nerissa, Portia's lady-in-waiting. A letter from Venice throws a shadow on Bassanio's happiness: Antonio seems lost; all his ships are wrecked. Shylock insists on the fulfillment of the ghastly contract.

Bassanio leaves in all haste for Venice in order to help his friend. Portia has a plan; together with Nerissa she also leaves Belmont, giving the care of her house to Lorenzo and Jessica who had arrived with the bearer of the bad news.

The three months have passed. Antonio has been incarcerated. Shylock demands his pound of flesh. In vain the Doge of Venice has tried to restrain Shylock. The law must take its course.

As a last resort, the Doge has asked a famous scholar of the law to make a judgment in the case. This person does not appear himself but a young judge, accompanied by a very young clerk, will act in his name. These two are the disguised Portia and Nerissa. Portia urges Shylock to drop his bloodthirsty demand. Bassanio offers triple the amount owed, but Shylock insists on his right; the law must not be offended. The young judge acknowlededges this to the great satisfaction of the Jew, who is already whetting his knife to cut the pound of flesh out of Antonio's body. Then Portia sets a surprising trap for Shylock. He may cut out the pound of flesh, but not an ounce more or less, and only the flesh, not a single drop of blood. Shylock is checkmate; he has to renounce his revenge and, moreover, is accused of intending to kill a fellow citizen. His possessions are confiscated; he leaves a broken man.

The supposed young judge and his clerk decline payment; all they want are the rings of Bassanio and Gratiano which these had received from their brides-to-be; with subtle words they manage to purloin them from their intended husbands who do not see through their disguises.

The last act brings everyone together in Belmont where Lorenzo and Jessica are waiting for their return. A playful quarrel about the rings and a joyful outcome conclude the play.

Music and evil

In the mantle of a moving, many-colored, tragic-comic drama the poet clothes the mystery of music. Music sounds at the critical moment when Bassanio makes his choice of the three little caskets; music prepares the return of Portia and Bassanio in the last act. There, in the moon-drenched park of Belmont, while the spectator already knows the happy outcome of the judgment, Lorenzo speaks with Jessica about the essence of music. We are lifted into the sphere of wisdom carried by love, from which this entire drama is woven. For Lorenzo's rich eloquence and Jessica's one touching, simple sentence "I am never merry when I hear sweet music" is not merely a pretty interlude that, after the fiercely dramatic fourth act, is intended to put the spectator into an idyllic mood; it is the quintessence of the entire story that is spoken here. The story leads us alternately into two domains: Venice and Belmont; and Lorenzo speaks of two worlds of music:

Sit, Jessica: look how the floor of heaven
Is thick inlaid with patines of bright gold:
There's not the smallest orb which thou behold'st
But in his motion like an angel sings,
Still quiring to the young-eyed cherubims;
Such harmony is in immortal souls;
But, whilst this muddy vesture of decay
Doth grossly close it in, we cannot hear it. [5.1]

A heavenly harmony of the spheres lives in the movement of the gold-gleaming stars. In the immortal souls of human beings this same music is enclosed, but we do not hear it because the perishable, "muddy" sheath of our body "doth grossly close it in."

Two worlds: a realm of origin, of light, life, and love, of vivid harmony and warm intelligence; Belmont, the fair mountain, Portia's realm; and a dark realm of hatred and passion, of grief and death: Venice, Shylock's realm. But here, in Venice, also lives Antonio, the offering heart. He is truly the principal figure after whom the play is rightfully named, for in the world of the "muddy vesture of decay" he carries the noble power of love which enables Bassanio to enter into his connection with the light realm. Antonio's sacrifice places him in direct opposition to evil. In the temporal world evil has its task; after all, Shylock's gold provides the material basis of Bassanio's success. But the evil one turns against the human heart, the organ that is the most immediate expression of the immortal soul in which, according to Lorenzo, the same harmony is alive that lives in the moving stars. Music restrains evil; hardened in evil is he who is untouched by the "concord of sweet sounds."

Listen to Lorenzo's continued speech:

Jessica:
I am never merry when I hear sweet music.

Lorenzo:
The reason is, your spirits are attentive:
For do but note a wild and wanton herd,
Or race of youthful and unhandled colts,
Fetching mad bounds, bellowing and neighing loud,
Which is the hot condition of their blood;
If they but hear perchance a trumpet sound,
Or any air of music touch their ears,
You shall perceive them make a mutual stand,
Their savage eyes turned to a modest gaze
By the sweet power of music: therefore the poet
Did feign that Orpheus drew trees, stones and floods;
Since nought so stockish, hard and full of rage,
But music for the time doth change his nature.
The man that hath no music in himself,
Nor is not moved with concord of sweet sounds,
Is fit for treasons, stratagems and spoils;
The motions of his spirit are dull as night,
And his affections dark as Erebus:
Let no such man be trusted. Mark the music.[5.1]

Shylock is "the man that hath no music in himself," whose soul sensations are dark as in the underworld. In the second act he orders his daughter: "But stop my house's ears, I mean my casements." He does not want the sounds of the music made by the nocturnal festive partygoers in the masked parade to penetrate into his "sober house," and entice the soul of this house, Jessica, to the openings of windows and doors.

In contrast to the strict orders Shylock leaves with his daughter, by which she is banished into the dark seclusion of the "vesture of decay," we hear Lorenzo's homily on the music of which she becomes part in the light realm of Belmont.

Just as the drama of the ancient Greeks, Shakespeare's drama was born from the spirit of music. However, because he lived in Christian times, he was able to show in a more immediate form that catharsis leads to victory over evil. Lorenzo's words about music are permeated through and through with ancient Greek wisdom; they proceed directly from Greek traditions. But the dramatic confrontation of the anti-music force with the sacrificial force of Antonio is post-Greece; it is in the deepest sense Christian and modern.

Before going into this further we must first return to the contrast of Belmont with Venice in order to make this convincing image even more transparent.

Belmont, the sun realm

Shakespeare's universal spirit must have had a deep affinity for the spiritual reality of Greek mythology. His poetical intuition penetrated into the very core of that world. England in the time of Elizabeth I and James I shows a culture that is deeply permeated by a humanistic spirit inspired by the Renaissance. Shakespeare stood completely in his time and intensively participated in this culture. But he succeeded, on the one hand, in giving the ancient world a contemporary appearance—he wrote for theater audiences, not for philologists. On the other hand, he knew how to make his dramatic pictures pervious to suprasensible reality, something which neither his fellow poets nor the scholars of his time were capable of. It is as if his genius had found the portal to the spiritual realm of the ancient temple mysteries, from which proceeded all mythology, all poetry, all culture of antiquity. And this is at the same time the secret of his modernity, for our culture today is asking in a modern sense for access to this realm of the spirit. After the discovery of the subconscious life of the soul, humanity in our time wants to penetrate more deeply, down into the regions of the original "harmony in immortal souls," which is one and the same as the spiritual harmony of the world-all. Shakespeare is a guide on this path.

Commentators on *The Merchant of Venice* have frequently, out of false notions, emphasized the incoherence of the play. A judgment that speaks of "fairy tale motifs combined with horror nonsense inspired by medieval anti-Semitism" is in every respect incorrect. The contrast between Belmont and Venice is in no way a more or less clever combination of different stories cobbled together from here and there to present a well-known theme to his public in a new and patched-up form. Between Belmont and Venice there exists a polar relationship, a coherence of the highest order that is the golden thread of a perfect composition. One principal aspect of this polarity has already been mentioned: Belmont is the realm where the harmony of the spheres reveals itself in all its radiance; Venice represents a world where everything is "muddy" and transitory, where the immortal soul is banished, threatened by evil, and has to suffer. This suffering of the soul in the oppression of earthly existence causes the "sadness" of which Antonio speaks to his friends. With the first sentence of the drama: "In sooth, I know not why I am so sad" the theme is opened which develops from scene to scene, until the sadness has been metamorphosed into joy.

The polarity between Belmont and Venice is characterized by the role played by gold in both regions. Shakespeare's text leaves not a grain of doubt that in Belmont only the spiritual power of gold has significance, while in Venice gold demonstrates its material necessity but also, due to its outer importance, stirs up a limitless egotism. Of old, gold was recognized in its relation to the sun. The sun too has an outer, blinding aspect and a deeper spiritual core. Belmont is in reality the image of this spiritual sun realm—no symbol or allegory, but a mythological imagination peopled with figures who, precisely in their living authenticity, reveal the ideal forces of which they are the bearers.

What is the secret of the sun realm? It is no coincidence that, in two places, Shakespeare makes a connection between the Lady of Belmont and the Golden Fleece. In the first act Bassanio describes the lady's enchanting being:

> ... and her sunny locks
> Hang on her temples like a golden fleece;
> Which makes her seat of Belmont Colchos' strand,
> And many Jasons come in quest of her. [1.1]

Then in the third act, when the right choice has been made, and when Gratiano has with less effort than his friend conquered the lesser girl (Nerissa), he exclaims: "We are the Jasons, we have won the fleece" (3.2).

The tradition of the Golden Fleece points to the existence of an esoteric stream in Greek culture. When the Greco-Latin cultural epoch takes its course on earth, the equinox is in the constellation of Aries, the Ram. The equinox (the highest position of the sun on March 21) moves very slowly through the twelve constellations of the zodiac. Many thousands of years before the Greek era the sun had also passed through Aries. In that far distant past humanity was still able to experience the direct revelations of the divine world. At that time, all culture, of which no physical traces exist, but which lived on in the memory of the ancient peoples, was permeated with primeval wisdom. We find the memory of this primeval wisdom in sagas and myths in many different imaginative forms. One of these was the Golden Fleece, the fleece of a ram bestowed on the twins Phrixos and Helle. Greek heroes led by Jason, together known as the Argonauts, brought this golden ram's fleece to their homeland. However, in the later period of the Ram, the primeval wisdom could only be preserved in secret cultic centers. The participants in the expedition of the Argonauts are to be considered as founders of such centers, also called mysteries.

Why were these centers of primeval wisdom surrounded by secrecy? It is a question of the greatest importance for our contemplations. Divine wisdom about the cosmos and the human being was originally connected with love. To preserve this connection between wisdom and love, the mysteries had to insist on an extremely strict schooling on the part of their adepts, consisting of purification, catharsis of the egoistic life of desire. For this life of desire had developed into a demonic counter-image of divine love due to the progressive darkening of earth-oriented humanity. Side by side with this esoteric wisdom stream, an outer stream of the culture of the intellect, philosophy, and science developed in Greece, which could be attained without purification of the passions.

Bassanio's conquest of Portia is an exact picture of the attainment of a higher stage of humanity, and the motif of purification is actually the real theme of the drama. We must not be misled by the playful final scene which makes it evident that the happy couples of Belmont in no way intend to be content with platonic love. This healthy sensuality, which we so deliciously meet without complexes everywhere in Shakespeare, is not at all inconsistent with ideal reality.

We should notice that the poet of *The Merchant* treats the purification process dramatically in such a way that it is distributed over the adventures of different characters. His mastery enables him to do this without a trace of allegory. Every character on the stage is authentic, also in a realistic-psychological sense. Bassanio wants to unite with Portia; he seeks the sun realm of Belmont where wisdom and love are united. In order to do this he has to leave his friend Antonio behind in the other realm with a heavy burden. Bassanio's rise to the sun realm fetters Antonio more tightly to the death forces of the lower world. By Antonio's total willingness to make this sacrifice the purification is achieved. Only this is able to make the union of Bassanio and Portia real.

The power of the sun realm now pulls Antonio up out of the world of hatred and death: Portia liberates him. Then Bassanio himself has to endure a test, for the young judge does not want ducats as his recompense, only this little strip of gold, the ring that sealed the connection of the two lovers. What else can Bassanio do but give the ring, on which he had sworn an oath of faithfulness, to his friend's savior whom, by the way, he had not recognized? And then the most beautiful, most noble wisdom of Shakespeare lights up: Bassanio receives the ring back out of the hand of Antonio.

In Jessica we also see an aspect of catharsis brought to life. In the soft luster of the moon her loveliness stands beside the beaming Portia. This leads us to another secret of the Belmont-Venice polarity.

The moon and the law

The opposite pole to the sun realm of Belmont is Venice, where moon forces are working. Medieval humanity was still quite familiar with the connection of the Old Testament with the moon and the New Testament with the sun. In our time, such distinctions have been lost. That is the reason why people have difficulties with the figure of Shylock; it is the reason why Shakespeare is accused of anti-Semitism. The poet shows us the Semitic figures that he puts on the stage in two aspects. On the one hand there is the noble, gentle Jessica, of whose being the foolish Launcelot gives us a telling picture: "Most beautiful pagan, most sweet Jew"; and on the other hand we have her father, the tough usurer Shylock. Here we have a sketch of two sides of Jewish nature, which not only are realities when considered historically and psychologically but which, against the background of the dramatic subject of *The Merchant*, also reveal deep spiritual connections.

The great mission of the Jewish people begins with the patriarch Abraham. In him, for the first time in human evolution, the capacity of abstract thinking is revealed. According to Jewish legendary tradition, he is the inventor of the art of arithmetic. This abstract thinking is dependent on the physical instrument of the brain which functions as a reflector. The reflective consciousness experiences the divinity no longer in mighty pictures, but holds in itself, in a spiritual-abstract manner, an imageless god.

This high, hidden god, whose name is Jahweh, relates to the One who is called in the Old Testament the Most High God, and whose priest is the mysterious Melchizedek, as the moon relates to the sun. The sun priest Melchizedek offers the moon priest, Abraham, bread and wine, the sacrificial substances of the Christ being. Abraham honors Melchizedek and acknowledges him as his superior. Thus we see a moon stream making its appearance in humanity that, in its beginning, reveals a spiritually subordinate relationship to the sun being. The most noble tradition of the Jewish people remains true to this subordination, until from the distant descendants of Abraham that most pure "moon vessel" is formed—Jesus the son of Joseph and Mary—into which the Most High Himself can descend.

Inevitably, however, a counterforce also develops. The brain-bound intellect runs the risk of turning into cold, loveless knowledge. The moon, which reflects the sunlight like a mirror at night, can eclipse the sun during the day. Wisdom that does not become the virtue of giving, grows into usury. Why is Shylock so enraged at Antonio? Because Antonio lends money without making a profit; because he gives in order to help, and not to receive more for himself.

But Shylock is not the personification of this counterforce; he is no allegorical scheme. He carries in himself the dark, loveless, side of the moon stream. His being evokes the sinister atmosphere of the Pharisees and Sadducees during the trial of Jesus, but at the same time he has the tragic greatness of Jewry in the Diaspora. In the implacable logic with which he justifies his lust for revenge smolders the suffering of his people: "For suffering is the badge of all our tribe." In this regard the noble Antonio is not to be absolved from guilt either. However, the toughness of his behavior vis-à-vis Shylock does not conflict with the generosity and readiness to sacrifice, which are also parts of his character. A tolerant, all-understanding and forgiving Antonio would not have evoked the dramatic conflict. Shylock's thirst for revenge, his insane demand of a pound of flesh, the unfolding of his dark lust to destroy would have made a lifeless, abstract horror story without Antonio's aversion of the usurer. The fact that this aversion is not so much directed at Shylock's race as at his personality, in which the shadow side of the Jewish race comes to the fore with excessive strength, becomes abundantly clear in the play. And the fact that Shylock does connect Antonio's hatred with his being Jewish, in his famous words in the third act—"... and what's his reason? I am a Jew ..."—is testimony to Shakespeare's lofty impartiality. He excuses neither Antonio nor Shylock; he lets living individuals speak.

In the fourth act the contrast between the life-giving

sun realm and the death-carrying moon realm reaches a culmination in the words of Portia and Shylock during the trial. Shylock demands the execution of the devilish deed on the basis of the law: "I stand here for law." The sacred, God-given law is the central nerve of the Old Testament. By adhering to the law in strictness and purity, the Jewish people remained true to their task. The essence of the law is connected with the past. The strict person of the law can do no other than look back: present and future are oriented exclusively to what was once given and now continues to roll forward unchangeable, inviolable. This reproductive character of the law, again, is deeply rooted in the being of the moon. The stream that carries heredity and, with it, the related, restricted morality of tradition, are wholesome as long as the direct relationship to the Godhead can still be experienced in it. Time and again, the leaders of the Jewish people, the high patriarchs, the touching figures of the prophets, restored this relationship when the danger lurked of estrangement from the Godhead. When estrangement takes place, the sacred law becomes an empty husk that will be filled with cold intellect and inhumanness.

The impulse of love turns away from using the law in this manner; only the true law can be fulfilled and renewed by love. Love does not reproduce; it creates. Through love, morality becomes creative intuition. Unchangeable, eternal repetition, petrified rigidity that leads to death, these are stopped. "Love does not rule, it creates, and that is more," said Goethe in his Fairy Tale of the Green Snake and the Beautiful Lily. From the sun realm Portia brings the message of love and mercy. It is as if Orpheus were singing when she speaks her hymn to mercy:

Portia:
Then must the Jew be merciful.

Shylock:
On what compulsion must I? tell me that.
Portia:
The quality of mercy is not strain'd,
It droppeth as the gentle rain from heaven
Upon the place beneath; it is twice blessed;
It blesseth him that gives and him that takes:
'Tis mightiest in the mightiest; it becomes
The throned monarch better than his crown;
His scepter shows the force of temporal power,
The attribute to awe and majesty,
Wherein doth sit the dread and fear of kings;
But mercy is above this sceptred sway,
It is enthroned in the heart of kings,
It is an attribute to God himself;
And earthly power doth then show likest God's
When mercy seasons justice. Therefore, Jew,
Though justice be thy plea, consider this,
That in the course of justice none of us
Should see salvation: we do pray for mercy,
And that same prayer doth teach us all to render
The deeds of mercy. I have spoke thus much
To mitigate the justice of thy plea;
Which if thou follow, the strict court of Venice
Must needs give sentence 'gainst the merchant there.
Shylock:
My deeds upon my head! I crave the law, ... [4.1]

Shylock is too hardened; he rejects the divine mercy with the same words the Jews shouted at Pilate: "His blood be on us and on our children!" Then the contract has to be enforced.

We know from many of his tragedies into what depths of darkness Shakespeare was able to reach. He now places the spectator before an undisguised ritual of black magic, as this was practiced by the native tribes in Mexico: with a few quick cuts of the sacrificial knife they removed the heart or the stomach from a living human being. In Shylock's case it has to be a pound of flesh as close as possible to the heart—the difference is not essential.

But when Antonio, after he has already bared his chest and spoken the most noble words of farewell to his friend, is ready to pay Bassanio's debt "instantly with all my heart," Portia brings the release with such an unexpected turn that all darkness disappears in one stroke. Portia's moral imagination, the idea that had entered no one's mind in Venice, breaks through the law by following its letter to its ultimate consequence. Because Shylock's demand is taken to its absurd extreme, humanness triumphs. Evil chains itself in the rays of a higher logic.

Fancy dies

Many poets have been able to picture the demonic chasms of the human soul. But when they tried to put the summits of happiness and spiritual loftiness into words, they frequently lacked the necessary fire and strength. Shakespeare, however, is here as sovereign as in his evocations of darkness. The scene in Belmont, when Bassanio is united with Portia by choosing the third casket, has such a golden sparkle, is so wise and noble, so passionate and modest at the same time, that the listening and watching spirit is filled with the deepest joy. At this moment music sounds too, but how completely differently from the fifth act!

There it is as if Lorenzo is inspired to bring his profound speech about the essence of music out of the primeval ground of the starry night in which the mysterious moon appears. Just before, Lorenzo and Jessica had been speaking of lovers who sang of their longings in such moonlit nights. The dialogue becomes playful when they mention their own destiny and love, but the women they evoke are all tragic figures: Thisbe, Dido, Medea. Weaving between the two is an atmosphere of light melancholy and of intimacy that is momentarily broken by the burlesque appearance of Launcelot, but then in peaceful quietness descends into them again. The night begins to speak, and reveals the secret of the sounding cosmos outside, and the sounding cosmos inside the human being.

It is different yet kindred when, in the third act, Portia commands that music shall sound to accompany Bassanio's choice. Here we do not yet have the still intimacy, the adagio of the singing night. Portia is in a state of extreme tension, but her soul is music. It is as if her "little body, aweary of this great world" is not formed from the perishable loam that makes the sounding soul inaudible. She says:

> Let music sound while he doth make his choice;
> Then, if he lose, he makes a swan-like end,
> Fading in music: that the comparison
> May stand more proper, my eye shall be the stream
> And watery death-bed for him. He may win,
> And what is music then? then music is
> Even as the flourish when true subjects bow
> To a new-crowned monarch: such it is
> Are those dulcet sounds in break of day
> That creep into the dreaming bridegroom's ear,
> And summon him to marriage. [3.2]

Is it possible to express in words an experience of minor and major more clearly than Portia does here? And then sounds the mysterious songlet about "fancy":

> Tell me, where is fancy bred,
> Or in the heart, or in the head?
> How begot, how nourished?
> Reply, reply.

It is engender'd in the eyes,
With gazing fed; and fancy dies
In the cradle where it lies.
    Let us all ring fancy's knell;
    I'll begin it, —Ding, dong, bell.
All:
Ding, dong, bell. [3.2]

Immediately thereafter Bassanio speaks the decisive word that contains the core of his right decision: "So may the outward shows be least themselves."

Although Portia does not sing the "fancy-song" herself, we should imagine that the words, together with the melody, are the sounds of the condition of her soul. Fancy, the love that is born in the eye, nourished by the perception of outer appearance, lust, also dies in the eye. The death knell of fancy awakens in Bassanio's soul the higher power of perception which is born from head *and* heart. But also in Portia's soul fancy is vanquished. For her, Bassanio's reach for the leaden casket, in which her image is hidden, is also a breakthrough to a crystal-clear power of love:

How all the other passions fleet to air,
As doubtful thoughts, and rash-embrac'd despair,
And shudd'ring fear, and green-ey'd jealousy.
O love, be moderate, allay thy ecstasy,
In measure rain thy joy, scan this excess;
I feel too much thy blessing; make it less,
For fear I surfeit! [3.2]

The use of rhyme indicates that Shakespeare wishes to give this lyrical monologue, which Portia speaks aside, special emphasis. He shows the darkness of Shylock, the force of hatred, in its "ecstasy," its unbridled wildness. The power of love is checked by the modesty of the free "I." The theme of purification reveals itself again in a transition from minor to major. Doubt, despair, fear and jealousy evaporate: "O love, be moderate."

It is as if Shakespeare transports us to the land of the troubadours, the singers of courtly love. There also, measure and joy were the carrying forces of the highest love. But this wondrous purification of the soul, which the poets of the Provence strove for, led to unrequited love. Merely one chaste kiss and the gift of a ring sealed the connection of the troubadour with his lady. Is it different in Belmont? The "gentle scroll" justifies Bassanio's kiss; Portia gives him a ring. And does not their love initially remain unfulfilled as a result of the stormy course of events that occurs immediately after? The Antonio drama has to hit rock-bottom before love can be fulfilled after everyone's return to Belmont. In the sun realm the spiritual connection, that on earth can only be made by abstinence, is a genuine union:

Das Unzulängliche,	Here, the inadequate
Hier wirds Ereignis;	To fullness groweth;
Das Unbeschreibliche,	Here is wrought the ineffable,
Hier ist es getan;	Through heavenly love;
Das Ewig-Weibliche	The ever-Womanly
Zieht uns hinan.*	Draws us above.

Apollo and Dionysus

Ever since Nietzsche wrote *The Birth of Tragedy Out of the Spirit of Music*, we have known that Greek drama was born from the blending of the Apollonian and the Dionysian. *The Merchant of Venice* was written three hundred years before Nietzsche made his brilliant discovery. Nevertheless, this drama by Shakespeare shows in its images such a surprisingly exact evocation of the worlds

---

* J. W. Goethe, *Faust*, Insel Verlag 1998; English translation by Theodore Martin, Dutton 1971.

of Apollo and Dionysus, that we in this regard are able to trace again Shakespeare's incredibly deep connection with ancient Greek culture.

Lorenzo's words about the harmony of the starry spheres turn us to the world of Apollo, and we have already seen that Portia's home, light-filled Belmont, reveals the true traits of the sun realm, wherein the harmony of the spheres is concentrated. Not only does the "fair mountain" evoke the memory of the lofty place of Apollonian music, the whole description of the events in this Belmont realm—which is not to be found on any map—leaves no doubt as to its true nature. The spectator is transported into those regions from where at one time the Greeks were inspired to a clear and balanced conception of their humanity. Measure and temperance rule this world; false semblance, which leads to death and folly, is here vanquished. In the right casket Portia's image is hidden, the true appearance that leads to union with the reality of the spirit.

Portia's wise father had the image of his daughter covered in "meager lead." Why lead? Lead is the metal that tradition connects with the planet Saturn. The Greeks considered Saturn, or Kronos, as the representative of a primeval generation of gods against which the Olympians rebelled. The original essence of humanity, the image of the human being, however, must be sought in this Father world. The spiritual sun realm mysteriously incorporates the old Saturn force in itself.

Perhaps it is more difficult to recognize the Dionysian world in Venice. The exuberant masked parades that made the city so famous, and to which Shylock shows his whole-hearted aversion, may give us an external entry point here. But the connection is of a much deeper nature. In Greece, Dionysus belonged to the chthonic gods, which means that one had to travel a difficult path into the underworld to find the god's true being. As mystery godhead he is related to the Egyptian Osiris who also had to be found in the world of the dead. This journey into the underworld had to be accomplished during life by those who were initiated in the Dionysian mysteries. It was a path of initiation on which one was exposed to the greatest dangers and trials. The catharsis, the purification which was the fruit of the terrors one endured, brought the initiate into connection with an aspect of Dionysus called Iacchus, who bore the characteristics of a future-redeeming god.

The mythical images of the Hades trials have a variety of content. In Egypt we encounter the well-known scene of the deceased standing before a large pair of scales on which his heart is weighed. At the top of the picture in the Book of the Dead one sees the judges of the underworld. Beside the scales sits a monstrous figure consisting of an amalgamation of different animals. This monster would devour the heart if it did not measure up in the weighing. All the experiences of the deceased, and that which was able to lead him to union with the midnight sun, Osiris, would also be lived through by the soul that sought this union already during life.

Let us now take another look at the fourth act of *The Merchant*. The judges are sitting in a solemn row. Portia, carrier of the sun impulse, appears in disguise: a severe black hat hides her sunny locks. In the realm of trial she adopts the garb of this severe world. Bassanio and Antonio should in a sense be viewed as a unity, the human being tested in the purification process. Shylock carries the scales on which the pound of flesh, "nearest to the heart," must be weighed. The feather of righteousness, which Portia throws on the scale, saves the heart.

The catharsis is accomplished. The way to Belmont traveled by Bassanio and the way to the dungeon, the trial in Venice, traveled by Antonio full of "sadness"—the journey to Apollo where "doubtful things" and "shuddering fears" have to be overcome, and the descent into Dionysus's realm where suffering and terror are checked by the power of love—they converge. By a deed of sacrifice, sun and earth are united. What works into the earth as evil moon power is removed: Shylock disappears. Before the sun rises over Belmont, appears the kind moon as the lovely, mysterious soul of Jessica. The spirit of music begins to speak, the dream world becomes transparent, the harmony of the world-all and depths of soul becomes audible.

Many generations, now and later, will still feel their way through the riddle of the man William Shakespeare who had the capacity to bestow such profound wonders on us, but more and more Goethe's word will be confirmed: "... Shakespeare ... who is certainly a higher kind of being to whom I look up and whom I venerate."

2

A Midsummer Night's Dream

Philia and Neikos

The poet's truth

> The poet's eye, in a fine frenzy rolling,
> Doth glance from heaven to earth, from earth to
> heaven,
> And as imagination bodies forth
> The forms of things unknown, the poet's pen
> Turns them to shapes, and gives to airy nothing
> A local habitation and a name. [5.1]

These words of Theseus, Duke of Athens, with which he relegates the nocturnal forest adventures of the charmed and then un-charmed lovers to the realm of fables and folly, are often viewed as a masterful characterization of poetry. If this were true, we would have to wonder why Shakespeare put the characterization of his most sacred gift, poetry, in the mouth of the complacent, intellectually rationalizing Theseus. But of course: it is only Theseus's truth that is proclaimed here and not Shakespeare's truth!

A large part of the theater audience—in Shakespeare's time just as much as today—may feel reassured by this Theseus truth. After all, the pictures that are shown in the dream of a midsummer night are just the fabrications of a poet, aren't they? Poets are considered on a par with the insane and with lovers—a category of people

27

whose "imaginations" must not be taken seriously. But in the thoughtful words with which Theseus's bride, Hippolyta, replies to her long-winded spouse there sounds a different truth. She says:

> But all the story of the night told over,
> And all their minds transfigur'd so together,
> More witnesseth than fancy's images,
> And grows to something of great constancy;
> But, howsoever, strange and admirable. [5.1]

The other truth, the truth of the poet, is not put in Hippolyta's mouth as wisdom. She merely indicates what is made visible by means of the magic of imagery in the entire dramatic action: "all the story of the night told over."

Art does not amount to giving form to "airy nothing." The creative imagination clothes the figures of the transitory earth with "forms of things unknown," meaning with spiritual reality, and therefore the transient earthly seems to turn into "something of great constancy." The creative imagination, the capacity of the poet, indeed connects heaven and earth—here Theseus is right—but what he calls "airy nothing" is rather the reality of a higher order that irradiates our "world of local habitations" and makes it "admirable."

In this passage, Shakespeare creates a contrast between "imagination" and "fancy's images." The latter are phantoms that come and go; imagination, however, is the spiritual eye that perceives a lasting higher reality. But this truth had to be hidden.

Why was Shakespeare so anxious to convince his public that the dramatic images of his play were but shadows, unreal like dreams in the night? Listen to Puck's epilogue:

> If we shadows have offended,

Think but this—and all is mended—
That you have but slumber'd here
While these visions did appear.
And this weak and idle theme,
No more yielding but a dream,
Gentles, do not reprehend;
If you pardon, we will mend.
And, as I'm an honest Puck,
If we have unearned luck
Now to 'scape the serpent's tongue,
We will make amends ere long;
Else the Puck a liar call:
So, good night unto you all.
Give me your hands, if we be friends,
And Robin shall restore amends. [5.1]

The puritanical spirit of Elizabethan times could very easily be offended by a show in which elves, fairies, Pucks and such were brought onto the stage. Popular belief in such nature spirits was looked upon as papist and strictly censured, even prosecuted by the City Fathers of London. A poet who brought such characters on the stage, therefore, had to be extremely careful. The time had come when anything supernatural had to be banished from human thinking, feeling, and belief. In Holland, for instance, the poet Vondel was mercilessly attacked by the Municipal Council of Amsterdam because of his angel play *Lucifer*.

When we today watch the delicious scenes of *A Midsummer Night's Dream*, we rarely realize that with this innocent, sparkling creation the poet put his life in jeopardy. For the City Fathers were not at all gentle in their measures against superstition or any convictions with which they disagreed. And poets and actors had a bad reputation in this regard.

Shakespeare, therefore, had a lot at stake with the creation of this comedy, but he protected himself from the "serpent's tongue"—an expression that might not just refer to hissing by the audience, but also to a condemnation by the authorities—by pretending that everything was but an airy fabrication without any basis in reality. For more than four centuries now, Theseus's ideas about poetry and Puck's roguish apology at the end have made fools of the reader and spectator.

But the time has come when we, in defiance of Puritanism and rationalism, have to follow in the footsteps of imagination in order to discover the "forms of things unknown." Modern consciousness is asking for a widening of its field of vision; the supernatural can no longer be pushed aside as "airy nothing" now that more and more people are suspecting that our current dead-end culture is in need of a breakthrough to spiritual territories.

Those who carry this as a presumption or as certainty in themselves will discover in the work of Shakespeare an astonishing wealth of spirit, not in a philosophical-theoretical form, but in an imaginative form that is of the greatest importance for human beings today. Shakespeare was still able to draw on old spiritual traditions and esoteric streams of his own time, but much more important than the influences he underwent from his contemporaries, writers of antiquity, and popular tradition was the relationship to spiritual realities he had as an individual. This relationship expresses itself in what A.C. Harwood called his "prophetic mind." The prophetic power of his spirit enabled him to give what has lived in humanity from time immemorial as mystery wisdom such a form that the old seems to be submerged in a spring of rejuvenation. And the rejuvenation was so strong, and carried such a powerful seed, that these works of poetry were able not only to survive the materialistic times in which the notion of spirit had become lost, but could even serve as a beacon of consolation. Now is the time to bring the rejuvenated mystery treasures in Shakespeare's work fully into light. I will attempt to make a contribution to this with the following study of *A Midsummer Night's Dream*, and will begin by giving a brief sketch of its content.

The dream of a midsummer's night

Act I

Theseus, Duke of Athens, is about to marry Hippolyta, the fair queen of the Amazons, whom he has vanquished in a battle. Shortly before the wedding, which is to take place at the beginning of a new moon cycle, Egeus, a prominent Athenian, comes to the court with a complaint about his daughter Hermia and her lover Lysander. Egeus has destined the pretty, dark-haired girl for Demetrius who desires her as his wife, although he was initially engaged to Helena. Hermia defies her father and confesses her love for Lysander before the whole court. She says she would rather die than marry Demetrius. Theseus's judgment is strict: she must resign herself to the will of her father, and if not, she will either be killed or spend the rest of her life as a sterile "nun of Diana."

Lysander consoles his beloved and arranges with her to escape from Athens. They will meet in the forest outside the city so they can go and live happily elsewhere. Helena, who envies her friend Hermia for her beauty, which holds Demetrius prisoner, is made part of the plan. She decides to tell Demetrius so that he will at least be grateful to her. She will follow him when he goes to the forest to look for Hermia.

A group of Athenian artisans are planning to perform a play called *Pyramus and Thisbe* at the occasion of the wedding of Theseus and Hippolyta. Their first rehearsal is to be held in the forest outside the city.

Act II

In the forest, Oberon, the king of the elves, and his spouse Titania are having a painful disagreement. They disagree as to the possession of a very beautiful little Indian boy. Titania does not want to give the child to Oberon. She reproaches her spouse that their disagreement has upset the harmony in all of nature. Oberon wants to insist. He orders Puck, his roguish servant, to fetch a little plant, the sap of which he will press on the eyes of Titania when she is asleep. Upon awakening, by the power of Cupid that burns in the sap, she will burst into flaming love for the very first masculine being she sees.

In the meantime, Oberon witnesses Helena's pain when she is rejected in the most cruel way by Demetrius, who is looking for Hermia. Oberon pities the poor girl, and, when Puck brings him the little plant, he tells him to use the sap on the Athenian youth as soon as the latter falls asleep.

Titania retires for the night; her elves sing a lullaby to her. Oberon presses the sap onto her eyes and utters the wish that she may behold a monstrous being when she wakes up.

Lysander and Hermia are fleeing through the forest. They are tired and lie down on the moss—at a chaste distance from each other—to go to sleep. Puck sees the slumbering Lysander and, thinking that this is the Athenian youth he is looking for, presses the sap onto his eyes. Helena, wandering about in her loneliness—Demetrius has run away from her—finds Lysander, who wakes up and falls head over heels in love with her. She thinks he is mocking her and runs away. He goes after her, leaving Hermia behind, who wakes with a nightmare. In despair because Lysander is gone, she goes into the forest to look for him.

Act III

The artisans are having their rehearsal in the forest close to the spot where Titania is slumbering. Puck watches the clumsy proceedings for a while and then, to play a trick on them, he changes the head of Bottom, the silliest of the lot, into the head of an ass. The disconcerted actors flee in a panic while Puck chases them up hill and down dale. Bottom thinks that they are pulling his leg and stays put, passing the time with a song. Titania wakes up and bursts into ardent love for the shaggy figure. She calls her elves together and, enraptured, takes her darling further into the forest.

Oberon is quite content when he hears of the state Titania is in; then Hermia and Demetrius enter. She reproaches him in most bitter words that he has killed Lysander. Demetrius professes his innocence, but Hermia runs away in a rage. Disheartened, Demetrius lies down to rest. Oberon is furious with Puck because the latter has made a mistake. Oberon wants to set things right: he drops the Cupid sap onto Demetrius's eyes. When then Helena appears, followed by an infatuated Lysander, Demetrius wakes up. The first person he sees is Helena, and now both men are in love with the girl who at first was spurned. She is deeply offended, thinking that both of them are mocking her. Hermia comes in and throws her arms around Lysander. He pushes her roughly away, for he is now in love with Helena. Bitter words are heard between the two former girlfriends; taunts and challenges between the overheated men.

Puck is having fun, but Oberon thinks the jokes have gone too far. Things have to be made good again. Puck is told to chase the crazy fighters so hard through the dark forest that they collapse from exhaustion. Then

Lysander's eyes have to be wetted with another sap, from the "bud of Diana," which will counteract the effect of the first sap. This will also be used to cure Titania after she has willingly relinquished the Indian boy. Puck perfectly executes his orders: the two fighters are deluded in the darkness until they indeed collapse from exhaustion; the desperately wandering girls also arrive at the place, and soon, unaware of each other's presence, the loving couples are lying on the forest floor, neatly arranged two by two, in deep sleep. Lysander's eyes are sprinkled so that he, freed from his delusion, can find his true love again.

Act IV

Titania has put a wreath of flowers on the head of her darling ass. She takes him to her bower. The elves have to serve him. They fall asleep. Oberon liberates his queen of her delusion; earlier, conscious of her pitiful condition, she had already relinquished the Indian boy to him. Puck takes the ass head off Bottom.

Early in the morning Theseus and Hippolyta come to the forest to hunt. It is their wedding day. They find the four lovers, who can hardly believe the fearful dream they had during the night. Egeus demands the penalty for his runaway daughter, but when Demetrius assures him that he loves none but Helena the wrathful father gives in. Theseus gives orders for the celebration of a threefold wedding that day.

Bottom is the last one to wake up. He has also had a weird dream—no one will ever believe what he dreamed. His mate Quince has to compose a ballad to that, and he will recite it at the festivities for the duke.

In Athens the artisans are at their wits' end. Their friend Bottom has still not come home, and who is now to play the role of Pyramus? No one can do it like he. While they are sitting together all disheartened, in comes Bottom joking and twaddling as usual. They can do the play!

Act V

Theseus and Hippolyta are speaking about the strange adventures of the pairs of lovers. The newlyweds join them, and the master of ceremonies offers them a list of recitations and stage performances to shorten the evening hours of the wedding night. They choose the tragic farce *Pyramus and Thisbe*. The exceedingly ludicrous show, in which the actors surpass themselves, provokes many merry comments on the part of Theseus and his guests. A little dance concludes the show, and the three bridal couples retire.

Puck enters and prepares the audience for the arrival of Oberon, Titania, and their following of elves. The palace is blessed with song and dance by these good spirits, and wishes for goodness and happiness are spoken for those who are united in love. Puck speaks the epilogue; he hopes for a big hand—for after all, wasn't it just a dream?

The moon sphere

Like the "Forest of Arden" in *As You Like It*, the forest outside Athens is no ordinary wood. It is the place where the dream vision of the midsummer night is enacted, where there are three groups of people who enter into a particular relationship with each other. In *As You Like It* also, the wood is a place of encounter, entanglement, trial, and catharsis. In Shakespeare's later plays—*Pericles, The Winter's Tale, The Tempest*—the sea coast takes the role of the symbolic forest, for there also the scenery has more of an imaginative than a literal character.

If in *The Merchant of Venice* Belmont represents the sun realm, we have in the Athenian wood certainly landed in a moon world, not the moon as the target of astronauts, but the moon sphere as the realm of the four elements, the sphere where vital forces are working.

The concept of "moon sphere" has no scientific meaning for modern human beings; they consider this word as a poetic expression or ancient superstition. For us, the moon is the physically visible satellite of the earth. Between the earth and the moon there is a virtually empty space of some 240,000 miles that can be traversed in a rocket. In an earlier age, however, science—which had then no less value than ours but a different nature— still recognized spiritual influences emanating from the heavenly bodies. The moon sphere, or other planetary spheres, were not understood as empty spaces that separate the planets from the earth, but as spiritual "territories" that permeate our world of the senses and in which certain spiritual beings work. The processes that take place in nature and in the human being were thought to be regulated by these beings. In the very distant past, human beings were still able to perceive the working of nature beings and planetary spirits in themselves and in the surrounding nature. Over time, however, the human constitution changed, and with it human consciousness changed, so that the ability to perceive such beings was lost. In mythologies, sagas, and fairy tales we find the reflection of what was once living experience. Gradually, the light of tradition also dimmed, and abstract thinking was only able to discover natural laws where formerly living spirit was known to exist. Understandably, the old wisdom then had to be set aside as superstition.

The pre-Socratic nature philosophers in ancient Greece still tried to incorporate in their teaching about the elements remnants of an older mystery wisdom of the life of the earth and the cosmos. In most of their works spiritual beings have already been reduced to abstract concepts; sometimes, however, the controlling forces were still called gods or demons. The contemplations of Empedocles (495-435 BCE) on the connection and dissolution of the four elements as a result of love and conflict—*philia* and *neikos*—may strike modern human beings as strange. But what in old times was generally known has today become strange for us. We come to know the world by analyzing its dead constituent parts. The Greek was still aware of the living processes that work in the relationships between things and focused more on the spiritual-qualitative in nature than the quantitative. Greeks did not arrive at knowledge by measuring and weighing such as we do, but by sensing the vital forces in one's own organism, which were related to the life forces in nature. Active influences akin to moral forces were seen as moving causes in life. Because of his own choleric temperament, Heraclitus felt that fire was the origin of all things, while the phlegmatic Thales recognized water as such.

The elements, therefore, were not hydrogen, nitrogen, oxygen, carbon, etc., arranged according to their atomic weight in the periodic table; they were earth, water, air, and fire. With the word *earth* we should not just think of sand and rock, but all that consists of solid substance. *Water* was everything that is fluid; *air* the gaseous condition; *fire* was not only that which was burning, but indicated all warmth processes. Moreover, early Greek natural science focused especially on the effects of these elements in the whole of nature, their mutual relationships, and their ideal nature. Nature was still an area in which cosmic forces were experienced, and this supranatural play of forces was perceived together with sense observation.

But it is not so much in Greece, but in the even more ancient Arian population of India, that we can find the connection between the moon sphere and vital forces, especially in liquid processes. For the Vedic Indian, the *soma* ritual was particularly essential. *Soma* was the sap of a plant. People who drank this sap after it had been fermented became intoxicated, which was experienced as a heavenly ecstasy; a higher consciousness, therefore, was also called *soma*. But *soma* also indicated the moon. Soma-moon was the regent of all fluid movement that had to do with strength, health, growth, and procreation in the rain, the waters, the realms of plants and animals, and also in the human organism. Soma consciousness enabled the ancient Indian to leave the, to him, unreal world of the senses (maya) and feel himself connected with a higher world of paradisal life forces:

> We have drunk soma and become immortal,
> We have attained the light,
> The gods discovered.
> Now what may foeman's malice do to harm us?
> What, O immortal, mortal man's deception?*

It is interesting that the Sanskrit word *soma*, which means heavenly life force and ecstatic consciousness, became the Greek word for *body*.

Let us now go back to the Athenian wood and listen to Oberon and Titania when the latter says to her spouse:

> ...Why art thou here
> Come from the furthest steep of India?

And a little later, when Oberon has asked her for the little boy whom he wants to have as a "henchman":

> Set your heart at rest;
> The fairy-land buys not the child of me.
> His mother was a vot'ress of my order:
> And, in the spiced Indian air, by night,
> Full often hath she gossip'd by my side;

---

* Rigveda Hymn 48 Soma verse 3, tr. Ralph T. H. Griffith, 1896. Source: sacredtexts.com/hin/rigveda/index.htm

And sat with me on Neptune's yellow sands,
Marking the embarked traders on the flood;
When we have laugh'd to see the sails conceive,
And grow big-bellied with the wanton wind:
Which she, with pretty and with swimming gait,
Following—her womb then rich with my young squire—
Would imitate, and sail upon the land,
To fetch me trifles, and return again,
As from a voyage, rich with merchandise.
But she, being mortal, of that boy did die;
And for her sake I do rear up her boy,
And for her sake I will not part with him. [2.2]

It is clear: the king and queen of the elves have their residence in far away India, the image of which is evoked in the quoted passage: moonlit night, the water element, fertility. By their presence in the Athenian forest this place becomes the scene of their influences. The supernatural and the natural mingle: mortals and immortal "little people" enter into relationships with each other. A dream arises that has more reality than down-to-earth reality. The moon sphere becomes visible. The poet serves us the soma drink of his word and imagination, and we fall asleep to the ordinary world in order to awake in a higher world.

Shakespeare makes us a little bit clairvoyant, for he shows us the moving causes that rule in the living realm of the moon sphere. These are moral forces, sympathy and antipathy, love and hatred, that bring about connection and dissolution.

In the first act already, even before the "dream," there is tension, polarity. On the positive side, Theseus has vanquished Hippolyta in battle, out of which their love has blossomed; on the negative side, Hermia's love for Lysander is thwarted, and Demetrius hates Helena whom he loved at first. Out of love, Helena betrays the secret plan of Hermia and Lysander to escape, which results in so much hatred and conflict. In the last act, back in the ordinary world, *philia* appears to prevail—the happy couples are all harmoniously united—but the play of *Pyramus and Thisbe* shows us that *neikos* has not yet been completely vanquished. The tragic death of these lovers is, however, suffused in so much mildness and humor that *neikos's* sting has been overcome.

The timing of the wedding of Theseus and Hippolyta is determined by the phase of the moon; the death of Pyramus and Thisbe is illumined by "moonshine." Without any doubt the actual principal character of the play is the moon; it exerts its influence in a variety of forms, first of all in Hippolyta, Queen of the Amazons. These warlike women worshipped, in addition to Ares, the god of war, the great mother goddess Cybele, who was an earth-moon goddess. According to ancient tradition, the famous mystery temple of the moon goddess Artemis (Diana) was founded by the Amazons. The Amazons, who were not really a people but rather a kind of order, a mystery community, took the principle of gynecocracy (the right of the mother and government by women) so far that they despised men and restrained erotic forces with extreme measures. The Greek heroes who fought the Amazons—Heracles, Bellerophon, Theseus—were representatives of the patriarchal principle that is related to the sun. Thus we hear Theseus earnestly admonish Hermia:

> To you your father should be as a god;
> One that compos'd your beauties, yea and one
> To whom you are but as a form in wax
> By him imprinted, and within his power
> To leave the figure or disfigure it. [1.1]

The penalty for her disobedience to her father's will is that she will be killed, or she must "abjure for ever the society of men." The Amazons' idea is thus represented by Theseus as an abhorrence. He warns Hermia to consider whether she will be able to live like "a barren sister all your life, chanting faint hymns to the cold fruitless moon." Theseus does praise those who succeed in thus controlling their blood that they preserve their virginity, but:

> ...earthlier happy is the rose distill'd,
> Than that which, withering on the virgin thorn
> Grows, lives, and dies in single blessedness. [1.1]

Higher than chill abstinence is the full-blooded acceptance of the connection a man and a woman enter into in marriage. Theseus's sentence on Hermia's willfulness is expressed in words that are once more a victory over the one-sided moon principle of the Amazons. Hippolyta is silent; she has been tamed and is ready for her marriage with the sun hero Theseus, but the expression of her face betrays displeasure, which explains Theseus's words: "Come, my Hippolyta: what cheer, my love?" (1.1)

At the end of the fourth act, Theseus and Hippolyta appear in the forest at sunrise. Hippolyta stands there armed with bow and arrow as the perfect image of Artemis, the goddess of the hunt and of the moon.

Helena also is entirely moon-like. She is pale and a little languishing beside the lively, dark-haired Hermia. Her beauty receives praise, but she longs to clothe herself in Hermia's beauty, just as the moon clothes itself in the light of the sun. Speaking of Demetrius, Hermia says: "His folly, Helena, is no fault of mine," to which Helena laments: "None, but your beauty: would that fault were mine!" (1.1)

The name Helena is the same as Selene, Greek for the moon, and the story of Helen of Troy indicates that the Greeks could not do without the moon-being Helena, the representative of beauty, artistry, and fantasy in their intellectually oriented culture.

Finally, the queen of the elves, Titania, is a moon being par excellence, and her name is surely related to that of Diana (Artemis). More than Oberon, who does not shun the light of the sun, she is a night spirit. Under her guidance the nature beings do their blessed work primarily in the plant realm, and her nature is more akin to that of the goddess Natura than to the capricious, teasing character of Queen Mab, as described by Mercutio in *Romeo and Juliet*. She grieves for the disturbance in nature caused by her disagreement with Oberon. Although, according to Oberon, she is in love with Theseus—as Oberon is with Hippolyta—her relation to mortals is different from that of her spouse. The latter appears to have compassion on human destiny, while Titania's principal concern is for the life of nature. Her worst punishment is therefore to fall in love with an ass's head. The ass—astrologically identical with Cancer—is in sagas and fairy tales the image of the physical body that is inaccessible to a higher world. An example is Midas who rejected Apollo's music: he was punished with ass's ears.

The scene of the slumbering Titania, entwined in love with the shaggy dunce, is the most poignant picture of the whole midsummer night's dream. Bottom, although he knows how to express himself like a gentleman, is really a silly clodhopper who does not leave the advances of the lovely little queen unrequited out of noble restraint, but out of plain obtuseness. He wants to eat dried peas and someone has to scratch his hairy head. Peas and beans were forbidden to the Pythagoreans because this heavy fare made any esoteric schooling impossible.

We spectators laugh at this droll spectacle, but aren't we all Bottoms with our illusory wisdom which, in regard to a supernatural world, could be much like the stupidity of an ass? And the poet, behind the mask of Puck, secretly laughs at us: Is it a dream? Is it reality?

The little people of the elements

Although India is the birthplace of the lunar wisdom of life processes, and, according to the text, Oberon and Titania like to tarry there, still Oberon as King of Fairyland is no oriental figure. The general view is that Shakespeare derived the name Oberon from "Auberon" in the Carolingian epic *Huon de Bordeaux*.

In this story Oberon is a pretty little, fairy-like being that possesses great magical power. Huon, who is traveling through the forest of Auberon, knows that he must not utter a word to the little elf king, so as not to fall into the greatest danger. After many obstructions and trials put in Huon's way by the magical powers of the elves, the story ends with an intimate friendship between him and Auberon. The little creature reveals his wondrous parentage: none less than Julius Caesar was his father and the fairy Morgue (Morgan le Fay) his mother!

Later commentators of the epic did not take Caesar's fatherhood seriously and went in search of the origin of the noble and helpful elf king. It was not difficult to identify him with the Germanic Alberich from the *Edda* and the *Nibelungenlied*, even though this dwarf has a malevolent character. We find the elf king also in other Germanic stories, always possessing some magical object (a stone that quenches one's thirst, for example). A French researcher, De la Villemarqué, however, claims to have found Auberon in the Celtic world, where his name is Gwyn-Araun or Gwenn-Aron. *Gwyn* means white (*albus, aube*) and *araun* indicates a supernatural being. Some researchers make a connection between the name Auberon and *aube*, dawn, and Shakespeare's text in the third act gives strong support to this view:

> I with the morning's love have oft made sport;
> And, like a forester, the groves may tread
> Even till the eastern gate, all fiery-red,
> Opening on Neptune with fair blessed beams,
> Turns into yellow gold his salt-green streams. [3.2]

In Celtic tradition Gwynn-Araun appeared like lightning from a cloud and was brought up by the fairy Morgan. Gwyn shows the same traits of generosity and helpfulness vis-à-vis human beings as Auberon. As does the latter, he possesses an ivory horn the sound of which makes everyone sing.

Oberon's servant Puck, or Robin Goodfellow, has his origin in the folklore tradition of Shakespeare's birthplace. Puck, although he shows some malicious traits—he likes to tease, just like Queen Mab—and also works with the magical powers of his master, is still presented as a spirit who brings goodness and happiness.

Thus we see the supernatural visitors of the Athenian wood as a group of spirits who are apparently gathered together from near and far, from Greece, Scandinavia, Brittany, and England. They are not forged together as a perfect unity by Shakespeare's genius alone. The Indo-Germanic peoples share a common primeval history, which reveals itself in the affinity of their mythologies, despite all their characteristic differences. As the creator of a new mythology, Shakespeare did nothing other than accurately restore the original relationships.

After all of this we might wonder: should a modern person now really believe in elves and goblins again? With all respect for Shakespeare and in spite of all wisdom from former times, may we not presume that these forces and beings exist only in primitive imagination and not in actual reality?

Obviously we must not fall back into belief systems of past ages. But we could perhaps consider the following: suppose that humanity in prior ages was not so primitive and superstitious as we sometimes think, and assuming that a sovereign spirit like William Shakespeare did not form his imaginations out of "airy nothing," how could we then in our current consciousness achieve a new and appropriate access to such spiritual worlds?

For many people the question may have no meaning, because they are firmly convinced of the correctness of our current materialistic picture of the world. Others, who are less prejudiced, may perhaps be willing to entertain the question. Only when one has taken the first steps in this direction does it become clear how much sense it makes to occupy oneself with this aspect of the world.

One can find information about the elemental world as the field of activity of nature spirits in the modern spiritual science of Rudolf Steiner. Out of his exact and trained clairvoyance Steiner presented an extensive picture of the field of vital forces which, as a suprasensible realm, penetrates the material-physical world. He called this the "elemental realm" or the "ether world." The human organism is also built up and maintained in its living form by such a complex of form-giving life forces, which should be distinguished from the purely mechanical forces of the physical world.

This distinction was lost in modern natural science as a result of the molecular and atomic way of viewing the world. So long as we insist on finding the principle of life in ever more complex molecular structures, the concept of "life force" will remain tossed on the heap of superstition, until a spiritual-scientific approach to the phenomenon of life can break through so that it can complement and correct materialistic theories.

The forces of life and form cannot directly be perceived through the senses. But a purely phenomenological approach to nature, such as Goethe practiced, in which all theorizing tendencies of the intellect are held back, and in which thinking is also developed as a sense organ for the ideas that work in nature, can take us a long way into the suprasensible realm of life forces. It is for this reason understandable why Rudolf Steiner grounded his spiritual science in an extensive study of Goethe's natural scientific method.

However, direct perception of life forces can only be achieved if higher sense organs have been developed. In this regard phenomenological natural science can only be a preparation; the organs for suprasensible perception have to be opened by systematic training. The idea that human beings, besides their normal senses, possess higher organs of perception that do not become active until they have been awakened, is just as absurd to a rationalistic view of life as the existence of nature spirits. Discussions on this point are fruitless. Those who wish to insist on rejecting such things will not be convinced by solid arguments.

But if one has overcome the skepticism of rationalism, one's reluctance, one's irritation, all of which keep us imprisoned in our time—as soon as the reality of spirit dawns in the mind, then wide perspectives are opened on the path of spiritual-scientific practice. One then discovers that the higher worlds become "things of great constancy" without a trace of sentimental airy-fairyness or suggestion. And it is only in the light of these higher worlds that our earthly world becomes, at least to some extent, comprehensible.

In relation to our contemplation of *A Midsummer Night's Dream* it is extremely interesting to hear how one can arrive at perception of the suprasensible world of life forces. Rudolf Steiner described the exercises that lead to this as follows. With the greatest possible concentration and surrender, one should direct one's attention to a particular physical phenomenon, such as the blue of the sky, the green of a meadow, the white of snow. If this is done with the necessary intensity and for a longer time, a moment will come when the outer color disappears and the soul is filled with a certain mood that has a moral character; for instance with blue it is the mood of religiosity. In this way we could let the most diverse sense impressions work in us. We could thus make disappear, in a certain sense, what we perceive around us through our senses, so that this veil of the senses is lifted. We would become conscious of moral experiences of sympathy and antipathy everywhere.*

I have already pointed out that for the Greek nature philosophers the effects of the four elements were determined by moral impulses, for instance, for Empedocles these were love and conflict. In Shakespeare's *Midsummer Night's Dream* too, these same forces, love and conflict, which connect and dissolve, are the true motivators in the action of the drama. It seems to me that this is the most important aspect of the play; not the fact that there are elves and gnomes in it, for without the ground-motif of love and conflict these would remain mere folkloristic curiosities. It is the genius of Shakespeare's imagination that he takes off the "veil of the senses" and thus reveals the moving causes of the realm of life forces. What is presented as a "dream" is then an awakening to the background of the physical events, and this background turns out to be the alternation of antipathy and sympathy.

Now, there is of course a difference between a true imagination of the elemental world, as this can be

---

* Rudolf Steiner, *Spiritual Beings in the Heavenly Bodies and in the Kingdoms of Nature*, CW 158, Anthroposophic Press 1992.

achieved through spiritual schooling, and Shakespeare's imaginations. In spiritual training we start with an intensive observation through the senses which has the character of a meditation; then the image disappears, and a moral mood fills the soul. Out of this it becomes possible, after a longer or shorter period of time, to perceive spiritual beings in the elemental world. The poet, however, puts people of flesh and blood on the stage in the roles of Oberon and Titania. The spectators watch those with their ordinary eyes, but the suprasensible arises as *appearance*; not deceptive appearance, but beautiful, therefore true appearance.

This is the principle of all genuine art, and it is the reason why art was and is always the interpreter of a "higher" world. Genuine art such as the art of Shakespeare, therefore, can help human beings find the way to the realm of the spirit. The reproducing artist, the director, the actor, who wish to do justice to the work of art, which means to let it rise to its level of imagination, has to have a degree of familiarity with this realm of the spirit. When this is not the case, the result will be a merely realistic, at best psychologically acceptable rendering which may be impressive because of its virtuosity, but may also evoke abhorrence because of bad taste, spurious special effects, or plain blunders. For instance, a performance in which Puck and the elves have to move following the directions of a ballet choreographer makes a queer and unnatural impression. The movements of these beings should actually be observed in the reality in which such nature spirits exist. If a director has no relationship with such things, he or she will, if they are honest, have no idea of what to do with the little people in the Athenian wood. A good actor can often still make something of Puck, but the elves usually fail miserably.

Love and conflict: the doctrine of Empedocles

A Midsummer Night's Dream was written in 1594 or early 1595. Shakespeare was then 30 years old. At that age already, his genius as a poet, his exact imagination, was fully developed. With remarkable courage and also a certain mischievousness he brought to the public a piece of spiritual reality, the world of the fairies. He rejuvenated the early Greek nature philosophy in the images of a charming comedy in which the alternation of love and conflict is shown as enchantments in a forest. Although he leads us from an initial disharmony to the eventual harmony of the threefold wedding—where the comical dissonant of the dying lovers Pyramus and Thisbe only serves to strengthen the joyful connections of the ending—still, the deeper significance of the love-conflict motif remains hidden. It is not until his last dramas that Shakespeare becomes able to fathom the deeper layers of this mystery. I will return to this in the chapters on the later plays.

Moreover, the love-conflict motif is not the only key to the *Midsummer Night's Dream*. The flower sap of Cupid and the equally powerful herb of Diana, which were sprinkled on the eyes of Titania and Lysander, introduce an important additional theme that gives the *philia-neikos* motif a more complex appearance. In order to clarify the relation between these two motifs it is necessary to go a little deeper into the doctrine of Empedocles that we have already mentioned.

Empedocles said that the primeval unity of all that exists is composed of the four elements fire, air, water, and earth. In the world of existing things and beings, the opposing powers of love and conflict, in ceaseless struggle with each other, bring about coming into being and perishing, unity and multiplicity, harmony and disharmony. The condition of harmony, which grows under the reign of love, is called *sphairos*; later thinkers called the opposite condition, in which *neikos* predominates, *akosmia*.

Shakespeare gives a striking picture of the *neikos* effect in the words of Titania when she describes the consequences of her struggles with Oberon:

> And never, since the middle summer's spring,
> Met we on hill, in dale, forest, or mead,
> By paved fountain, or by rushy brook,
> Or in the beached margent of the sea,
> To dance our ringlets to the whistling wind.
> But with thy brawls thou hast disturb'd our sport.
> Therefore the winds, piping to us in vain,
> As in revenge, have suck'd up from the sea
> Contagious fogs; which, falling in the land,
> Hath every pelting river made so proud
> That they have overborne their continents:
> The ox hath therefore stretch'd his yoke in vain,
> The ploughman lost his sweat, and the green corn
> Hath rotted ere his youth attain'd a beard:
> The fold stands empty in the drowned field,
> And crows are fatted with the murrain flock;
> The nine men's morris is fill'd up with mud;
> And the quaint mazes in the wanton green,
> For lack of tread are undistinguishable:
> The human mortals want their winter here;
> No night is now with hymn or carol blest—
> Therefore the moon, the governess of floods,
> Pale in her anger, washes all the air,
> That rheumatic diseases do abound:
> And thorough this distemperature we see
> The seasons alter: hoary-headed frosts
> Fall in the fresh lap of the crimson rose;
> And on old Hyems' chin and icy crown
> An odorous chaplet of sweet summer buds

Is, as in mockery, set: the spring, the summer,
The childing autumn, angry winter, change
Their wonted liveries; and the maz'd world,
By their increase, now knows not which is which:
And this same progeny of evils comes
From our debate, from our dissension:
We are their parents and original. [2.2]

From the description of the continual struggle between love and conflict we could be led to conclude that Empedocles considered the process of world becoming and world passing away as a rhythmical alternation that is, in itself, unchangeable and eternal. This process looks different, however, when we take Empedocles's mystical teaching into account side by side with his nature philosophy. The mystic and the nature philosopher in Empedocles have often been considered as two irreconcilable sides of his being. Ernest Renan called him a mixture of Newton and Cagliostro; Wilhelm Capelle, more justifiably, compares him with Faust, for just as in Faust, the natural scientific and mystical aspects of Empedocles's philosophy are closely related.* As a mystic, the philosopher longs to find in himself the divine primal unity. The striving of the soul that has ripened to insight can only be to conquer its entanglement in what has become its pollution by the lower. *Neikos* has chained the human soul to isolation, to evil. But *philia* can reawaken the divine that has died in world becoming. Human beings can wake up the god in their souls; they are able to do this because they are themselves divine. Only like can know like, said Empedocles.

---

* Ernest Renan (1823-1892), French philosopher and author of *La Vie de Jesus* (The Life of Jesus); Wilhelm Capelle (1871-1961), German author who wrote the standard work *Die Vorsokratiker* (The pre-Socratics); Alessandro Cagliostro (1743-1795), an enigmatic Italian who studied alchemy, Kabala, and magic.

This is how the perhaps strange sounding divinity of Empedocles, which he proclaims of himself and which was acknowledged by his contemporaries, should be understood in the light of the old mystery initiation. In the Egyptian mysteries also, the murdered, dismembered god Osiris was reborn as Horus from *Philia*-Isis; and the pharaoh was by his initiation reconnected with the originally divine ground of the world: he became a god. The initiated, deified human being can work as a healer among humanity. This was said also of Empedocles. A preserved fragment of his work follows:

> O friends, ye who inhabit the great city of sacred Akragas up to the acropolis, whose care is good deeds, who harbour strangers deserving of respect, who know not how to do baseness, hail! I go about among you an immortal god, no longer a mortal, honoured by all, as is fitting, crowned with fillets and luxuriant garlands. With these on my head, so soon as I come to flourishing cities I am reverenced by men and by women; and they follow after me in countless numbers, inquiring of me what is the way to gain, some in want of oracles, others of help in diseases, long time in truth pierced with grievous pains, they seek to hear from me keen-edged account of all sorts of things. But why do I lay weight on these things, as though I were doing some great thing, if I be superior to mortal, perishing men?

But this state of deification is born only out of suffering and pain:

> Friends, I know indeed when truth lies in the discourses that I utter; but truly the entrance of assurance into the mind of man is difficult and hindered by jealousy.*

---

* Empedocles, *Fragments and Commentary*, Arthur Fairbanks, ed.

To his pupil Pausanias he speaks:

> You shall come to know all remedies, as many as are in existence, that ward off illness and old age, because for you alone shall I fulfill all of this. You will calm the violence of the always blowing winds that throw themselves onto the earth and parch the seed in the fields. And on the other hand, you shall at will call up the winds that repair the damage. Out of dark rain showers you shall awaken drought that is beneficent to the people; but from the drought of the summer you shall raise tree-nourishing flowing waters that descend from heaven. And out of the world of the dead you shall raise up the life force of the deceased.†

The purified human being becomes a beneficent magician who is able to control the forces of nature out of his own insights for the wellbeing of humanity. And reading this text, aren't we reminded of the impressive picture of Prospero, the magician in Shakespeare's *The Tempest?*

When *A Midsummer Night's Dream* was written, however, Shakespeare was not yet able to portray the deeper mystical side of the love-conflict motif in his dramatic works. For that he first had to go through suffering and darkness himself. His great tragedies were yet to come.

In *A Midsummer Night's Dream* he still shows *philia* and *neikos* as blind powers which dominate both the lives of the little nature spirits and the soul realm of the human beings. And yet, through the entire play Shakespeare has woven a thread which here also represents the mystical element of catharsis. Let us now follow that thread.

---

and trans., London 1898. Hanover Historical Texts Project.
† Wilhelm Capelle, *Die Vorsokratiker*, Alfred Kroener Verlag, Stuttgart 1963 (tr. from Dutch by P.M.).

Twofold Cupid

Besides the force of true love, which leads to undivided harmony, to the union of that which by its origin belongs together, there operates another, powerful love principle that is capricious, demonic in nature. It is awakened by the transient beauty of a sensory appearance and evokes in the deeper regions of the soul life the forces of desire and passion that shackle the soul to the material. It is a seductive power because it conjures up what seems like the true being of love, but isn't. This is the love principle of Cupid or Eros. Only those who can see through its seductive effect and are able by abstinence and self-control to safeguard themselves from its shackles, can incorporate this principle of love into true love as a force that serves it.

But Cupid's power—for this oldest and yet youngest of the gods is deeply mysterious—can also light the fire of true love. Then he is not blinding, but he opens the eye that is touched by the splendor of the beauty of the beloved being, and in his sensory rapture he seals what is, by its own true nature, a suprasensory bond.

Those who overlook this double aspect of Cupid would have to run up against a curious contradiction in the *Midsummer Night's Dream*. Titania and Lysander have to be released from the influence of Cupid's flower sap that brought them to a state of infatuation and thoughtless passion, but Demetrius's eyes are reopened for his true love of Helena by this same sap. This contradiction dissolves when we recognize in Cupid not only an evil seductive power, but also the child of the heavenly Venus, Venus Urania.

It is evident that Oberon is familiar with the double effect of Cupid. For he wants to punish Titania by causing her to fall in love with a monstrosity, but the means he uses for this he also gives to Puck to make Demetrius fall in love again with his true beloved Helena. And this latter effect proves to be lasting, also after the trials of the night have passed.

In what way does the Cupid motif move and play through the "dream" world of the Athenian wood? When Oberon orders Puck to fetch the sap to punish Titania, he tells him the following:

> My gentle Puck, come hither. Thou remember'st
> Since once I sat upon a promontory,
> And heard a mermaid, on a dolphin's back,
> Uttering such dulcet and harmonious breath,
> That the rude sea grew civil at her song,
> And certain stars shot madly from their spheres
> To hear the sea-maid's music.
> *Puck.* I remember.
> *Obe.* That very time I saw—but thou couldst not—
> Flying between cold moon and the earth,
> Cupid all arm'd: a certain aim he took
> At a fair vestal, throned by the west;
> And loos'd his love-shaft smartly from his bow,
> As it should pierce a hundred thousand hearts:
> But I might see young Cupid's fiery shaft
> Quench'd in the chaste beams of the watery moon,
> And the imperial votaress passed on,
> In maiden meditation, fancy-free.
> Yet mark'd I where the bolt of Cupid fell:
> It fell upon a little western flower—
> Before milk-white, now purple with love's wound—
> And maidens call it Love-in-idleness.
> Fetch me that flower; the herb I show'd thee once:
> The juice of it on sleeping eyelids laid
> Will make or man or woman madly dote
> Upon the next live creature that it sees. [2.2]

With this description Oberon clearly evokes the negative aspect of Cupid. The song of the mermaid is like a sweet enchantment that, while calming the furious waves, causes certain stars to shoot out of their fixed courses and therefore stirs up disorder in the harmony of the cosmos. In this equivocal situation Cupid can aim his fiery arrow in the sphere that lies between the cold moon and the earth. His target, a fair vestal throned in the west—it is assumed that the poet referred here to Queen Elizabeth—is not struck, because "the chaste beams of the watery moon" quench the fire of the arrow. But the arrow falls on a little plant that since then was called "love-in-idleness." In Shakespeare's time, "idle" not only meant having nothing to do, but also unfruitful, barren, empty.

In the realm of nature, everything material is inherently bound to die, but it also contains an element of passion that is akin to love, and through which, out of matter, a renewal of life, procreation, comes into being.

Shakespeare's entire work is a witness to his insight that the elements of passion and delusion have to be overcome to make true love relationships between human beings possible. Among his contemporaries there were poets and spiritual seekers who considered all eroticism as pernicious, but Shakespeare's ideal—we have already heard it in the words Theseus speaks to Hermia—is not the rather theoretical absolute abstinence propagated in their works by people like Chapman, Lyly, and Northumberland. For Shakespeare, the temptation that is part of the negative Cupid aspect is a necessary stage that has to precede the true harmony of love.

Already before the beginning of the dramatic developments of the play, Demetrius had come under the power of Cupid, who had distanced him from Helena. That is clear from Helena's lamentation:

Love looks not with the eyes, but with the mind,
And therefore is wing'd Cupid painted blind.
Nor has Love's mind of any judgment taste;
Wings and no eyes figure unheedy haste:
And therefore is Love said to be a child,
Because in choice he is oft beguil'd.
As waggish boys in game themselves forswear,
So the boy Love is perjur'd everywhere;
For ere Demetrius looked on Hermia's eyne,
He hail'd down oaths that he was only mine;
And when this hail some heat from Hermia felt,
So he dissolv'd, and showers of oaths did melt. [1.1]

And now, what led to the conflict situation of the first act because of Demetrius's flighty nature—Lysander calls him a "spotted and inconstant man"—has to be brought back into harmony. Hermia and Lysander are also involved in this process; they also have to go through a trial, because in the end the harmony has to be the right equilibrium between all four people. The trial they endure, it is true, is caused by a mistake: Puck confuses Lysander with Demetrius. But in the back and forth of love and conflict chance proves to be an effective instrument that first mixes the loving couples up and then, chastened and tested, puts them back together more tightly. Lysander will find his way back to the fiery Hermia after he has been liberated from his passion for cool Helena by the cooling sap of "Diana's bud"; Demetrius has to return to his moon-like beloved Helena by the fiery sap of "Cupid's flower" that cures him of his fervor for Hermia.

Thus, with an almost Greek feeling for measure and balance, the poet conjures up before our eye the symmetry and crosswise entanglements of both his dramatis personae and his motifs. It is not only the work of Cupid, but also the influence of the moon that is shown in a double aspect, as a positive force of sympathy and negative antipathy. I have already mentioned that by her marriage to Theseus, Hippolyta, the Amazon, overcomes the one-sided, ascetic moon principle: for sterile chastity is just as one-sided as infatuation. This sterility led the Amazons to an uncompromising, ruthless element of fighting, which could only be vanquished by fighting. With the two loving couples also, like has to harmonize like: an uncompromising, ruthless love element—Demetrius's passion for Hermia—must be vanquished by the love sap.

In Shakespeare's works *A Midsummer Night's Dream* follows shortly after the creation of his tragedy *Romeo and Juliet*, and these two plays relate to each other in a remarkable polarity. In *Romeo and Juliet* a marvelously pure love blossoms in the shadow of death; *A Midsummer Night's Dream* shows us love in the dream of the realm of life, where the element of death takes the form of shackles to perishable matter: Titania's love for the ass. But this death element is veiled by humor, just as in the play of Pyramus and Thisbe which, although a parody, shows a surprising similarity with *Romeo and Juliet*.

Romeo and Juliet are called "a pair of star-crossed lovers," lovers crossed, thwarted by the stars, meaning, brought to ruin by destiny. We could call the lovers of *A Midsummer Night's Dream* "moon-guided," guided by the moon to their happy bonds. The untimely marriage of Romeo and Juliet leads to death; the moon magic in the Athenian wood leads the two loving couples merely through the nocturnal trial of delusion and conflict, in order to make their marriages possible at the right time.

3

MACBETH

Tragedy of Evil

Out, out, brief candle

> ...Out, out, brief candle!
> Life's but a walking shadow; a poor player,
> That struts and frets his hour upon the stage,
> And then is heard no more: It is a tale
> Told by an idiot, full of sound and fury,
> Signifying nothing. [5.5.]

These words, spoken by Macbeth when he hears that his wife has died, are the summary of his own life. Thereafter, senselessly raging in the battle he has already lost, he makes his last steps on "the way to dusty death." This chasm of disillusionment in life is not unfamiliar to us modern people. Even if we do not always possess the brutal honesty of the doomed Macbeth, we certainly recognize his philosophy of the totally senseless life, like suction emptying our soul.

What causes this emptiness? What brings human beings to the point of denying the meaning of life? What illness, what misfortune, what obtuseness can possibly lead them to this bankruptcy of their spiritual existence?

Knowing how to interpret the images of *The Tragedy of Macbeth* will help us find answers to these questions. Shakespeare, the great prophet of the New Age, shows us in the mighty imaginations of his most compact drama the disintegration of the human soul by the effect of evil. But likewise he shows which power, which force alone is capable of standing up to this effect.

The story

Act I

Three witches come together on a deserted moor. They speak about a battle that will be over by sunset. Then they will approach Macbeth.

There is a rebellion against King Duncan of Scotland. The rebels are supported by Normans, but Macbeth and Banquo, the leaders of Duncan's forces, succeed in defeating both the rebels and the Normans. Duncan receives the good news and orders the execution of the Thane of Cawdor who had committed treason. Macbeth is to receive Cawdor's title and possessions as his reward for the victory.

Macbeth and Banquo return from the battle. The witches are awaiting them and greet Macbeth with three titles: Thane of Glamis (the title he had already), Thane of Cawdor, and King. When Banquo encourages the drab creatures to predict his future too, he learns that not he, but his descendants will wear the royal crown. Macbeth wants to interrogate the witches further, but they are suddenly gone.

Messengers from Duncan arrive with the news that the dignity of Cawdor has been bestowed on Macbeth by the king. Twice therefore the witches spoke the truth; would the third greeting then not be fulfilled? The thought of murder enters Macbeth's mind, but he still rejects it: "If chance will have me king, why, chance may crown me, without my stir."

Macbeth and Banquo go to the king who receives them with gratefulness and honor. They will all go to the castle of Macbeth, who hurries ahead to notify his wife. He had already written her a letter describing his encounter with the witches and the prediction of his becoming king.

Lady Macbeth reads the letter and gives her ambitious thoughts free reign. A servant reports the approach of Duncan. Like a priestess of evil Lady Macbeth now invokes the powers of darkness to help her execute the murder of the king. When Macbeth comes in, she pours all the snake venom of her ambition into his already affected soul. Duncan is reverently and cordially received in the castle. But Macbeth slips away from the festive meal; he wavers and weighs the consequences of the contemplated evil deed. With burning words, Lady Macbeth once again succeeds in winning her spouse over to the planned murder.

Act II

It is late at night; the king is already asleep. Banquo and his son Fleance, accompanied by a torchbearer, are walking across the courtyard to their sleeping quarters. Macbeth enters and the two comrades in arms exchange a few words. Then Macbeth is alone. In front of him he sees a dagger suspended in the air with the hilt pointing to him. He reaches for it, but it is only a specter; the hand can't touch it. Drops of blood appear on both blade and hilt. In this starless night laden with crime, Macbeth invokes the solid earth, that she may not hear where his fatal steps are leading...

Lady Macbeth, who has intoxicated the guards of the royal bedroom with wine and sleeping draughts, is waiting in the courtyard until her husband has performed the murder. Macbeth comes back; the daggers of the two guards, with which he has stabbed the king, are in his bloody hands. He says he heard a voice saying: "Macbeth does murder Sleep." His wife reproaches him for his tenderheartedness. She takes the daggers back to the place of murder because Macbeth does not dare to do this himself. She smears the two guards with the blood of the murdered king to make it look as if the horrible deed was done by the drunken helpers. When she comes back her hands are also red with blood. There is loud knocking at the south gate. Macbeth stands lost in thought; his wife takes him to their bedroom.

A drunken doorman comes to open the gate with a large key. He drivels something about hell and devils and then offers the entering noblemen Macduff and Lennox his obscene drunkard's wisdom. Macbeth, who was awakened by the noise, indicates the bedroom of the king to Macduff so that he can wake him up for their departure. Horrified and loudly shouting Macduff wakes up the whole castle after he has seen the murdered Duncan. Duncan's sons, Malcolm and Donalbain, come running in; Lady Macbeth appears and so does Banquo. Macbeth returns from the room of the king. Furious because of this scandalous deed he has killed the two apparently guilty guards. Lady Macbeth faints. Malcolm and Donalbain suspect false play and decide to flee as fast as they can, before they also get the dagger. Malcolm goes to England, Donalbain to Ireland.

The next morning the Scottish nobleman Ross speaks with an old man, who cannot remember ever to have experienced a night with such violent weather. The atrocities of people unleash the fury of the elements. King Duncan's horses have broken loose in unimaginable savagery and have torn each other to pieces. Macduff comes in and reports that Malcolm and Donalbain are suspected of the murder of their father. Macbeth will be crowned King of Scotland. Macduff does not want to attend the coronation.

Act III

Macbeth is now king, but he is tormented by fear and

suspicions. For the witches predicted that Banquo's descendants will wear the crown. Banquo and his son Fleance have to be killed. He orders two desperadoes to do this.

A festive banquet is being served in the royal castle. The murderers enter with the report that Banquo has just been killed, but that Fleance has escaped. The spirit of the murdered Banquo appears at the table sitting in the still unoccupied place of Macbeth. The latter watches the bloody specter with abhorrence. Neither the guests nor Lady Macbeth are able to see the apparition; they only observe and hear the fierce perplexity of their king. The specter disappears, but the banquet is upset. The guests take a hasty departure. Macbeth and his spouse remain behind in the hall. They speak about Macduff who is giving no heed to the call of the king to appear at court.

Macbeth wants to visit the witches again so that he can learn more from them about the future. Hecate, goddess of calamities and death, warns the witches that Macbeth is coming. They should prepare for a dark magical ritual that will throw Macbeth further into perdition.

In the royal palace Lennox speaks with a Scottish lord. It clearly appears from their guarded allusions that they have a suspicion of the true facts of the murders of Duncan and Banquo. Macduff has left for England to ask the English king for help against Macbeth.

Act IV

In a cave the witches are busy preparing their black magical brew. Macbeth appears and adjures the sorceresses to answer his questions. He is shown three apparitions: *a helmeted head* that exclaims: "Beware Macduff!"; *a blood-covered child* that proclaims: "None of woman born shall harm Macbeth"; and *a crowned child holding a tree in his hand* who says: "Macbeth shall never vanquished be, until Great Birnam wood to high Dunsinane hill shall come against him." By these last two pronouncements Macbeth's mind is put at ease regarding his own destiny: for he is invulnerable to human threats, and no wood has ever mounted a steep hill to a castle. However, he wants to know more: "Shall Banquo's issue ever reign in this kingdom?" The witches reply: "Seek to know no more" but he insists. Then a procession rises up showing eight kings, the last one holding a mirror in his hand, followed by Banquo's spirit. Macbeth curses the day that this truth was shown him. The witches disappear.

Lennox, who had been standing guard outside the cave, reports that Macduff has fled to England. Macbeth decides to surprise Macduff's castle and massacre his wife, children and all the serving folk. This takes place; the murderers force their way into the hall where Lady Macduff is sitting with her little son. The valiant child who stands his ground is stabbed to death under his mother's eyes.

In England Malcolm and Macduff are speaking about the unbearable tyranny under which Scotland is suffering. Malcolm tests Macduff in order to see whether he will serve the good cause loyally and selflessly. The king of England, Edward the Confessor, a holy man who has healing powers, is willing to send his best general with ten thousand men to Scotland to put an end to Macbeth's evil deeds. Ross arrives with the news that Macduff's wife and children have been murdered. After words reflecting deepest pain and prostration, Macduff pulls himself together. He will meet the Scottish devil with sword in hand.

Act V

Macbeth has entrenched himself in Dunsinane castle. Lady Macbeth walks in her sleep. A doctor and a lady in waiting secretly listen to what the heavily laden soul of the queen utters: the abominable blood guilt of the royal couple.

The English army under Siward and Malcolm is marching on Dunsinane. The Scottish nobility joins the liberation army that has reached Birnam Wood. Malcolm gives the order that every soldier must cut off a leafy bough so as to approach the castle under its cover.

Remembering the apparitions in the witches' cave, Macbeth fancies himself invulnerable. Lady Macbeth's condition is alarming, and what the doctor had been afraid of now happens: she commits suicide. A messenger reports that Birnam Wood is moving toward Dunsinane. One half of Macbeth's sense of security is now lost, but "none of woman born" can harm him, right? These words too will turn out to be true *and* false. Outside the castle he engages his attackers; in a man-to-man fight he kills the young son of Siward, the English general. Then however, he faces Macduff who jolts him out of the delusion of his invulnerability with the words: "Macduff was from his mother's womb untimely ripp'd." Macbeth is killed and the avenger brings his severed head to the assembled victors. Malcolm is hailed as King of Scotland.

History

At first sight, it would seem that this tragedy, with all its scenes of medieval warfare, murders, specters and witches' conjurations has no relation whatsoever with the problems of modern people concerning the meaning of life. This relationship only becomes clear, however, if we begin to read and fathom the successive events in the story as expressions of a higher reality. When we do not just read the text attentively, but at the same time try to imagine the action in the space of a stage, the soul will come into a condition that can be compared with dream consciousness. With a good performance this happens to a high degree. Then we discover that these stage-dream-images have a depth of reality that transcends the seemingly realistic representation. However, Shakespeare possessed the capacity so to let this higher reality coincide with the lower that there is no trace of pretended symbolism in his work. This is why his dramas affect both reader and spectator so profoundly.

Before we move on to reading and interpreting these higher realities we have to devote a few words to the historical background of the drama.

The events take place in eleventh century Scotland, where a strong Celtic element was still living at the time. The Celtic culture, nourished in earlier times from primeval mystery sources, a powerful culture of druids and bards who possessed magical powers, had then already fallen into decay. Even today some sparse remainders of an atavistic clairvoyance are still living among the population of Ireland and the British Isles, in which a connection with nature forces, perceived as spiritual and demonic beings, still exercises a profound influence on human beings. In the eleventh century this was even more the case, and in Macbeth we see a human being who still carries these atavistic capacities in himself.

Such old capacities were good and normal in the early eras of the history of humanity, but as evolution progresses they become decadent, demonized. Macbeth's soul is receptive to visionary experiences, but these lead to his perdition because he is not able to find the transition to a new consciousness—a new kingship—in the right manner.

In the beginning of the play we hear of an attack by Normans, Germanic people therefore, who were carriers of a different culture than the Celts. For the Germanic peoples were destined to develop in the future the intellectual consciousness that had already awakened in the Greeks and Romans. This consciousness, from which all connection with spiritual realities has disappeared, forms the basis of our present culture.

The fact that Macbeth repulses the Nordic influence is highly significant. He is a figure who lives in the dangerous twilight between a once powerful past and an as yet indistinct, budding future. To be a real king he would have had to take into himself the force that was able to counteract the degeneration of the old picture consciousness, and transform this still half dreamlike spirituality. This force is the force of Christianity, which bestows on the soul that has awakened to intellectuality and consciousness of self a new connection with beneficent spiritual powers.

The sons of King Duncan, Malcolm and Donalbain, flee after the murder of their father. Donalbain goes to Ireland, Malcolm to England. The latter prince goes to England's King Edward the Confessor who provides him with an army to drive out the Scottish tyrant. Important in this connection is the fact, which is emphasized by Shakespeare, that the good English king has healing powers in consequence of his holiness. A Christian impulse lives and works in this king who also possesses "a heavenly gift of prophecy"; it is this Christian impulse that makes a deep impression on young Malcolm, and that guides him on his return to the dark world of Macbeth. I will come back to this later.

Fleance, Banquo's son, also flees when his father falls under murderers' hands. He goes to Wales. Later he returns to Scotland and becomes the patriarch of the royal house of the Stuarts. That is, Shakespeare states that as a fact. Historical research has, however, proven that this is not correct. *Macbeth* must have been written shortly after the coronation of James I, the first Stuart on the English throne. Even more than Elizabeth I, this remarkable king, who had written a book on demonology, was Shakespeare's patron and supporter. It is understandable that the poet wanted to honor the scion of the Stuarts with his Scottish, "demonological" tragedy. The error he made in reliance on incorrect historical sources in no way diminishes the grand conception of his drama.

The change in consciousness caused by the transition from the old visionary capacities to the modern intellectual consciousness took place in the centuries that separate King James I from King Macbeth. Early in the seventeenth century, Celtic Scotland and Germanic England were united; the new consciousness triumphed. Shakespeare echoed this victory. He did not rebel against the tendencies of his time, as Schiller and, in a certain sense, Goethe did. But his confirmation also pointed in a certain direction. Discovering this direction is for our time, in which the intellectual consciousness is developing *ad absurdum*, of great significance.

The three murders

In our attempt to fathom the higher reality of the dramatic pictures referred to above, we should note the three consecutive murders as salient points in the composition of the tragedy: the murder of the old King Duncan, the murder of the comrade in arms Banquo, and the murder of the wife and children of Macduff.

The murder of the king is committed at the urging of Macbeth's wife. She fans the fire of his ambition and will to power, overcomes his vacillation, and smothers the voice of his conscience. To the succeeding murders he is led by his fear of losing the royal power that he so fiercely desired and had perfidiously won. Lady Macbeth is no longer involved in these. His decision to kill the children comes after the visions in the witches' cave have intensely tormented him and, at the same time, stricken him with the blind delusion of invincibility. Duncan and, in a certain sense, Banquo also were standing in the way of his ambitious plans; but Macduff's wife and children are the victims of senseless bloody terror.

In three horrible steps humanness disintegrates. In the first two, Macbeth's soul is not yet completely hardened: he is still conscious of the atrocity of his deed, or this is shown to him in the appearance of Banquo's ghost. The third murder leaves him cold; he is filled with cynicism, rage and disdain for life. In the last scenes he goes to his end as a possessed monster.

However, when we rise from the psychological level to a higher "mythological" or imaginative level, the three murder scenes reveal their true, archetypal character. Old King Duncan was in fact a rather weak figure; Shakespeare, however, shows him as a good and wise father of his people. Imaginatively speaking, the murder of Duncan means a breach with the world of the *father*. Even the icy snake Lady Macbeth says: "Had he not resembled my father as he slept I had done't." Duncan is killed while he is asleep. Macbeth believes to have heard a voice that cried:

Sleep no more!
Macbeth does murder Sleep, the innocent Sleep,
Sleep that knits up the ravel'd sleeve of care,
The death of each day's life, sore labour's bath,
Balm of hurt minds, great nature's second course,
Chief nourisher in life's feast.
Lady Macbeth: What do you mean?
Macbeth: Still it cried, "Sleep no more!" to all the house:
"Glamis hath murder'd sleep, and therefore Cawdor
Shall sleep no more, Macbeth shall sleep no more!" [2.1]

By killing the old king in his sleep, Macbeth breaks his own connection with the salutary source of nourishment of life, the world of sleep, in which each human being every night is taken back into a condition of paradisal innocence. In order to become king, Macbeth tears himself away from the divine father world of which the good and wise King Duncan is the representative.

The scene in the courtyard of Macbeth's castle is a grandiose image of the *fall into sin*. The story of the fall into sin refers to events that took place in a far distant past in human evolution. Just as in the play, so also in the book Genesis we are without any doubt transported into an imaginative reality. The pictures relate that human beings, under the influence of certain spiritual beings—represented in the Bible as the serpent—prematurely developed a consciousness that enabled them to gain knowledge of good and evil. This means that human beings became severed from God; they received an "I"-being of their own through which, because it made self-consciousness possible, they became in a certain respect God's equals and obtained *freedom*. On the other hand, however, this severance, this isolation, had to be paid for with death and a receptivity to evil.

Human beings thus, one could say, wrongfully appropriated the kingship of the ego to themselves. This appropriation was a slow process that took place over long ages of development. As a result, in their day-consciousness human beings were less and less able to share in the world of their origin, the world of the divine wisdom and life-bestowing powers of light that had embedded and nourished them in paradise. Only in sleep do human beings return to the world of their spiritual origin for a brief time. But their waking "I"-consciousness must then leave them. Human beings cannot penetrate into the realm of the Tree of Life as long as their

"I"-consciousness fetters them to the sensory, perishable world.

In the old pre-Christian initiations that enabled certain individuals to restore their contact with the spiritual realm—the realm of the Tree of Life—the "I"-consciousness had to be completely suppressed. The mystery acts that led to such initiations were only possible if the personal freedom of the ego being was fully handed over into the hands of the hierophant (the leader of the initiation process). With the coming of Christ on earth a fundamental change took place in this regard. Christ enables human beings, *in the full preservation of their "I"-consciousness*, to find the *religio* again, their re-connection with the spiritual realm.

As I have mentioned, the process of severance from the divine father world occurred very slowly. In the course of pre-Christian cultures, the "I"-consciousness of human beings developed step by step. This development was in a remarkable way supported by the use of wine which at that time did not, as it does today, darken the "I" but, on the contrary, greatly stimulated it in those times. In the Dionysian intoxication, for instance, one rose into one's own "I"—one became en-thu-siastic, i.e., filled with godhood. But this inner "I" experience meant at the same time a breach with the world of the old gods. For the forms of the "mythological" consciousness, in which an unfree, dream-like connection with the divine world was still possible, changed; they became decadent. Human beings became citizens of earth; their eyes were opened more and more to the sensory, god-forsaken earthly world.

While the fall into sin was, in a certain sense, an elevation of humanity, we also observe that it caused human beings to come under the influence of demonic beings that have the intention of diverting them from their true destiny. The development of the ego resulted in the development of egoism. The life of passion and desire, the "hot blood," grew out of control. These forces of passion have always been pictured as animals or, as in ancient Greece, as half human, half animal. We should note, however, that these animal forces only show their negative aspect in the human soul that has become egoistic. Before the development of "I"-consciousness, animal images were used as expressions of lofty cosmic powers that worked from the regions of the stars. We still see this in the image of the centaur, which was viewed by the ancient Greeks as a wise teacher of heroes, but also as a being that was impelled by wild passion.

Earlier I called the second act of *Macbeth* an imagination of the fall into sin. Kingship lay in Macbeth's destiny, but he seized it wrongfully, prematurely. In the as yet immature and unpurified soul, seizing the "I" in this way works as a catastrophe that finds its reflection in an explosion of the elements and animal passion: the terrible weather during the night of the murder and the suddenly wild horses of Duncan that break loose and tear each other apart.

The drunken porter "jokes" about being the "devil-porter" of hell. He prates about the effect of wine that provokes lust. Some people have called this "comic porter" with his drunken drivel a lack of taste of Shakespeare (Schiller left him out in his Macbeth translation), but the "tasteless" text is certainly to the point in the picture I have sketched here: hell, devil, wine, lust.

The murder of Duncan takes up the entire second act. From the beginning there are two dominant motifs: the dagger and blood. First the horrible vision of the dagger:

> Is this a dagger which I see before me,
> The handle toward my hand? Come, let me clutch thee—
> I have thee not, and yet I see thee still.

Art thou not, fatal vision, sensible
To feeling as to sight? or art thou but
A dagger of the mind, a false creation,
Proceeding from the heat-oppressed brain?
I see thee yet, in form as palpable
As this which now I draw.
Thou marshall'st me the way that I was going;
And such an instrument I was to use.
Mine eyes are made the fools o' the other senses.
Or else worth all the rest: I see thee still;
And on thy blade and dudgeon gouts of blood,
Which was not so before. There's no such thing:
It is the bloody business which informs
Thus to mine eyes. [2.1]

Then, in Scene 2, Lady Macbeth:
I laid their daggers ready;
He could not miss 'em.

And after the murder has been committed:
Why did you bring these daggers from the place?
They must lie there. Go carry them, and smear
The sleepy grooms with blood.

Macbeth does not dare to go back. Lady Macbeth:
Give me the daggers.

Macbeth's hands are red with blood and so are those of Lady Macbeth; old Duncan lies bathed in blood; the sleeping guards are smeared with blood; after the discovery of the murder Macbeth kills them both—blood, blood, blood! Blood that cannot be washed off with all the water of the ocean; blood that tints all green seas red. And all the time the dagger. Lennox says after he has seen his horribly murdered king:
Those of his chamber, as it seem'd, had done't.
Their hands and faces were all badg'd with blood;
So were their daggers, ...

And later, Donalbain to his brother Malcolm when they decide to escape:

...Where we are,
There's daggers in men's smiles: the near in blood,
The nearer bloody. [2.2]

Blood is the instrument, the carrier of the human "I." It becomes guilty through egoism; it then turns against the blood of others. The "I" has received the freedom not only to distinguish, but also to do good and evil. It is a double-edged sword or dagger. The awakening intellect, in which the individual earthly "I" begins to work, cuts its connection with the world of sleep; the intellect continually murders the living Father in us. In his feigned sorrow for Duncan's death, Macbeth utters a deep truth, words that are a prelude to his cynical negation of life in the last act:

...for, from this instant,
There's nothing serious in mortality:
All is but toys: renown and grace is dead;
The wine of life is drawn, and the mere lees
Is left this vault to brag of. [2.2]

What we witness here is the first step on the path of decay and death; the first stage toward the bankruptcy of life. The imaginative reality of the murder of Duncan is clear: a violent severance of the lower ego from the original kingly wisdom and goodness. In the twilight of a declining imaginative consciousness the still immature ego force usurps the domain of the soul. "Sleep" has been driven out and, with it, the eye for destiny; the "dagger" rages on. From now on Macbeth has to wade in blood more and more. After the "heat-oppressed brain" comes the cold fear of the lonely, godless human being hardened in egoism.

The murder of Banquo which follows is prepared and

executed in a different way than the murder of the king. The effect can now only be perceived by Macbeth himself: no one but he observes the apparition of Banquo's spirit at the banquet. The storm that raged outside when Duncan was murdered now rages only in Macbeth's soul. This second phase takes place on a different level from the first.

The murder misses its most important target: Banquo is killed but his son manages to escape. The prediction of the witches regarding Macbeth's kingship comes true due to his own intervention; the prediction relating to Banquo's descendants will come true in spite of Macbeth's violence. He now does not want to take destiny in his own hands, but challenges it to the extreme:

... come, Fate, into the list,

And champion me to the utterance! [3.1]

The murder of Duncan was a horrible act indeed, but what followed from it, Macbeth's kingship, lay in the latter's destiny; only he seized it wrongfully, prematurely. Banquo's murder, however, is an attempt at breaking destiny. While the killing of the old king can be viewed imaginatively as the "vertical" severance from the father world, Macbeth's second crime is a violation of the "horizontal" bonds that bind one human being with another: a human brother is killed.

Macbeth's deed reminds us in certain respects of that of Judas, while the scene at the banquet where the spirit of the murdered Banquo appears, is the ghostly counter-image of the Last Supper. In the one case we see the Redeemer, ready for his sacrificial death, indicating his traitor, in the other the unredeemed specter of the murdered man, visible only to his perfidious human brother, indicating the guilty one after the fact. The resurrection from death, the deepest meaning of the sacrifice on Golgotha, is now by the cynical words of Macbeth in which he denies the ghostly apparition of Banquo, distorted into a dark counter-image:

> If charnel houses and our graves must send
> Those that we bury back, our monuments
> Shall be the maw of kites.
> ... The times have been,
> That, when the brains were out, the man would die,
> And there an end; but now they rise again,
> With twenty mortal murders on their crowns,
> And push us from our stools: this is more strange
> Than such a murder is. [3.4]

The third step, which leads to the complete disintegration of Macbeth's humanness, is prepared by the scene in the witches' cave in the fourth act. For immediately after, he gives the order to surprise the castle of Macduff and exterminate its inhabitants. The murder of the child, from which Shakespeare does not spare his spectators, may not be as exciting and oppressing, from a dramatic point of view, as the murder of the king and the scene at the banquet, but in the overall picture of the play this scene is of the greatest importance, also as an imagination.

Macbeth himself remains completely in the background; his sinister servants execute his command. But it is by this last, senseless crime that he loses all reality of life. He no longer has any future; and he cannot go back.

The child dominates the imaginative atmosphere of the entire fourth act. Two of the three visions in the witches' cave show a child, the blood-covered child and the crowned child holding a tree in its hand. Also, the figure of Macduff comes more strongly to the foreground. The well-known quack astrologer Simon Forman, who saw a Macbeth performance in 1611, spelled the name as

Mac Dove. The fact that the name of Macbeth's oppo-
nent means *son of a dove* should not tempt us to an all-
too-easy symbolic explanation. But that the figure of
Macduff hides a "spirit secret" is certain. He was not
born in a natural way; he is not "a man born of woman,"
but a "mac-dove," a spirit son. The meaning of the
witches' prediction is clear: not the natural, "sinful" part
of the human being engendered through heredity can
vanquish Macbeth, the representative of evil. Only the
part that is "not of woman born" can achieve this: the
spiritual being.

Macbeth is unable to reach this part; it is outside his
power. And for this reason he kills the children, just as
once Herod killed the children in his powerlessness.

Through three stages we have followed the disintegration of the human being and tried to understand the
imagery offered to us by the prophetic mind of the
poet. When does life lose its meaning for human beings? When they turn against the threefold ground of
existence. Humanity has gone the path of Macbeth: the
change in consciousness that occurred gradually, and is
still in process, takes us into the "sleeplessness" of the
"dagger intellect"; it leads us to believe in death-and-
there-an-end instead of in the resurrection and the life;
and it causes us to murder the child because we want to
destroy the spirit essence of the human being.

On the level of imagination the persons of the drama
are *together* the complete human being. In humanity
there are also other powers working, powers that overcome evil. In other characters of his tragedy Shakespeare
shows us the representatives of these powers of the good.
We will see that the child with the power of the Tree of
Life is the image of the Redeemer. However, before we

turn our attention to the side of light in this tragedy, we have to look even more deeply into the dark side.

Devil and Satan

Malcolm calls Lady Macbeth "the fiend-like queen" and indeed there are few among Shakespeare's dramatic characters who merit the epithet of the devil more than this woman. Her share in the murder of Duncan is decisive, and in the fifth scene of the first act she openly reveals her inhuman malevolence:

> Come, you spirits
> That tend on mortal thoughts, unsex me here,
> And fill me from the crown to the toe top-full
> Of direst cruelty! Make thick my blood,
> Stop up th' access and passage to remorse,
> That no compunctious visitings of nature
> Shake my fell purpose, nor keep peace between
> Th' effect and it! Come to my woman's breasts,
> And take my milk for gall, you murd'ring ministers,
> Wherever in your sightless substances
> You wait on nature's mischief! Come, thick Night,
> And pall thee in the dunnest smoke of hell,
> That my keen knife see not the wound it makes,
> Nor Heaven peep through the blanket of the dark,
> To cry: "Hold, hold!" [1.5]

When we view the murder of the king as an imagination of the fall into sin it is not difficult to recognize in Lady Macbeth the image of the serpent. She even says to her spouse:

> ... Look like the innocent flower,
> But be the serpent under't. [1.5]

Her hissing, whispered promptings fan the ambitions of Macbeth; she knows just how to play the strings of his mind so they will sound in tune with her unwavering will. She knows no compassion, no pangs of conscience, no fear or hesitation. She oversees the situation, prepares everything, corrects the mistake Macbeth makes by taking the daggers with him. With her demonic genius she manages the entire nocturnal operation. Even when Macbeth shows a little weakness by killing the two sleeping guards after the discovery of the murder, she saves the situation by fainting at just the right moment.

Deeply acquainted as he was with spiritual realities, Shakespeare could not let Lady Macbeth hold onto her role as the seductive luciferic demon in the further course of the drama. In the third act already she remains more in the background; moreover, she becomes more human. She does not cause the murder of Banquo; Macbeth leaves her ignorant of the "deed of dreadful note," even if his allusion is clear enough.

Why does the demonic aspect of Lady Macbeth decrease until, in the last act, we even begin to feel compassion with the tormented sleepwalker? Because her essential being, the representative of the luciferic serpent power, shows its archetypal character only at the fall into sin of the murder of the king. The murders that follow are not inspired by the luciferic spirit that, on the one hand, dominates human beings from inside like a scorching fire but, on the other hand, in severing them from the divine world, elevates them, makes the "king."

Starting in the third act, we begin to see a different motivator that impels to murder than blind ambition. It is the fear that is growing rampant in Macbeth's soul, fear of losing his crown, fear of the sterility of his wrongfully obtained kingship, fear for his life. He becomes possessed by fear, like Herod who had to make use of black magic in order to retain his power—for the tradition of the murder of the innocents in Bethlehem incontestably points to black-magical practices in which the Herodians were quite skilled.

Who is the inspirer of fear? Is there a person in the drama who gives form to this dark power, the way Lady Macbeth represents the serpent of ambition? We may of course think of the three witches and their mistress Hecate, but I am of the opinion that these figures have to be viewed in a different light. They do not in the true sense instigate things; they work like a catalyst in a chemical process.

It is evident that the evil power that drives Macbeth to the murders of Banquo and the family of Macduff has no direct representative as a person in the drama. In the extremely compact composition of the drama such a figure would really not be acceptable. Therefore, the poet shows the turn in the nature of the malevolence by sketching a change in the condition of Macbeth's soul at the beginning of the third act:

To be thus is nothing, but to be safely thus.
Our fears in Banquo stick deep. [3.1]

In the lines that follow, we hear the word *fear* twice more; thus three times *fear*: *our fears*, then *would be feared*, and *I do fear*. The first time it is the noun, then the verb in the passive form, then the active form reinforced by *I do*. Step by step Macbeth becomes himself the representative of evil. But the type of evil he represents has a different character from that of the "fiend-like queen." Here Shakespeare touches on the mystery of evil as such. Evil does not work in the world as a single power; it has a *double* aspect. There is the aspect of Lucifer, the devil, the tempter who works in the human being's life of hot passion and desire, the inspirer of pride, ambition, envy and lust; and there is the aspect of Satan, the dark liar whom the ancient Iranians called Ahriman. He is the lord of death and of the ice-cold intellect, the master of black magic and of the most absolute will to power, the enemy of all that is light, warm, noble, and love-filled.

Because he is the anti-love force, he inspires fear; fear fills the soul when it lacks love.

Although the mythological traditions of different peoples, and certainly Christian documents, admit of no doubt as to the double character of evil, precise knowledge of this was lost in the course of time, just as all old mystery wisdom was gradually lost. Even the deeply probing spirit of Goethe was not able to distinguish the devil from Satan. His Mephistopheles carries the essence of both united in one figure, even though in *Faust I* he shows a more devilish, and in *Faust II* a more satanic aspect. Compare, for instance, Mephisto's role in the tragedy around Gretchen with that of the inventor of paper money at the imperial court.

The medieval Christian devil is primarily luciferic-diabolic in character, but in the old Christmas plays from Oberufer* we can still observe a clear difference between the devil in the Paradise Play (the serpent) and the one in the Three Kings Play (the inspirer of the massacre of the innocents). We hardly need mention that with the rise of modern natural science, which is based on sensory observation and rational thinking, the idea of *devil* completely disappears and is relegated to the realm of fables.

In Shakespeare's time such spiritual traditions had not completely paled and had not yet been condemned and disposed of by the rise of rationalism. In protestant England, this was indeed the case with fairies, spirits, and other nature beings. But speaking of devils and angels was still considered Christian, and the strict Puritans even had a certain predilection for hell and devil. But there was only one devil, just as there was only one God. Believing in two "chief devils" would have been rejected

---

* These medieval plays were rediscovered by Karl Julius Schröer and brought to new life by Rudolf Steiner.

and condemned as heresy both by the Catholic and the Protestant churches.

But the genius of the poet never troubles itself about restrictions imposed by clerical, scientific, or other dogmatic authorities; he plunges straight down into the depths of the realities of life. The artist who draws from the well of truth finds the same spiritual realities that are revealed by the mythological imagery and religious documents of the different peoples, and which can also be rediscovered by a modern exact science of the spirit.

Macbeth is the tragedy of evil. The power of the devil appears on the level of imagination in the figure of Lady Macbeth, in full operation in the scene of the murder of the king, representing the fall into sin. The power of Satan does not appear in an imaginative form, but merely as a psychic reality in which the magical practices of the witches are a decisive factor. The luciferic-diabolical element works through a woman, the satanic through a man.

While in the Middle Ages the luciferic element predominated, with the dawn of the New Age the satanic, or ahrimanic, principle begins to manifest more strongly in the evolution of humanity, although in a much earlier phase it had already had a profound influence—witness the stories in the Celtic, Germanic, and Iranian mythologies.

Being a child of his time, Shakespeare was not yet able to present a clear picture of the being of Ahriman in his dramas, but out of his prophetic genius he could make its influence visible. Macbeth possessed by fear, the murder of his friend and companion, and the murder of the child speak clearly to the imagination. It is up to us contemporary humans to learn to comprehend this language for today, four centuries later, the ahrimanic principle has become enormously powerful in us human beings and in our culture. It may try to hide, just as evil always tries to hide, but we must recognize it. It hides behind the mask of materialistic science and technology, behind prosperity and progress, and behind many phenomena in our individual and social lives. But in all reality it is really the power that inspires anti-love that leads us to betray and kill our fellow human being, and that inspires us to kill the child as the herald of a spiritual realm of light. It is the huge power of the denial of life that whispers into our ear:

> Life's but a walking shadow, a poor player
> That struts and frets his hour upon the stage,
> And then is heard no more. It is a tale
> Told by an idiot, full of sound and fury,
> Signifying nothing. [5.5]

Hecate and the witches

In the preceding section about the double aspect of evil, the three witches and their dark chief Hecate have been largely left out of consideration. Yet it is clear that these figures play a central role in the "tragedy of evil." Shakespeare leaves us in the dark as to whether the witches are beings of flesh and blood or supernatural figures. Macbeth and Banquo see them as bony, weather-beaten, bearded women in shabby rags, hardly distinguishable from the earth-brown moor. Their sudden disappearance after their prophecies to the two warriors indicates a supernatural rather than a physical-sensory nature.

On the other hand, we hear from the first witch that she has begged a mariner's wife for chestnuts—a real, physical thing to do. The woman's refusal evoked her lust for revenge, which the witch directed to the seafaring husband. This revenge is of an obviously black-magical nature—witness the thumb of a drowned pilot—and therefore supernatural.

It is, however, a feature of witches that they are able to step out of their bodies in a certain way and can then work as demonic spirits. Therefore it does not need to be a contradiction when one moment they behave as physical, and then again as supernatural beings.

Over and above the question of whether they are real sensory beings or have to be viewed as suprasensible, at the mythological or imaginative level the witches have a significance of the greatest importance. This significance has to be considered together with the goddess Hecate. The scene in which Hecate herself appears (3.5) to call her headstrong servants to order and prepare them for the arrival of Macbeth, was without doubt not written by Shakespeare. This passage shows the clumsy style of a poetaster—maybe an actor who dressed up the tragedy a bit to please his sensation-loving public. It was common practice in those days that people added, rewrote or mutilated scenes without any respect for the original playwright. The texts were owned by a group of actors and they could do with them as they saw fit. Despite all this, the Hecate figure most certainly belongs in the play. Twice Macbeth uses the name of this mysterious goddess in authentic Shakespearian lines.

Serious study of Shakespeare's work leads to the conviction that allusions to Greek mythological pictures are never accidental additions or concessions to the fashion of his day. Greece was alive in him with elemental force. With faultless precision he uses the right mythological names to reveal the depths of the dramatic situation to those who know the spiritual reality of the mythological images.

In order to explain what the ancient Greeks originally meant with the goddess Hecate it is necessary to give a concise presentation here of a piece of spiritual science. It has already been mentioned that the development of human consciousness proceeds in phases that gradually pass from one to the next. In the far distant past, humanity possessed a sort of dream-like clairvoyance. They did not yet see the world in sharp outlines as we do, but images arose in them of an imaginative nature. Nature, climate, heavenly bodies still appeared to them as ensouled. Spiritual beings revealed themselves to them that lived and worked in the movements of nature. But in those times humanity still lacked what we call intellectuality. They did not yet think in concepts that represent the lawfulness of nature in abstract forms, nor did they experience themselves as closed, separate individualities vis-à-vis nature. As ensouled beings, people felt themselves one with the ensouled all around them.

The awakening capacity to think developed out of this mythological consciousness only when the human "I" connected itself more strongly with the earthly nature of human beings. This led human beings to distinguish between their own inner soul world and the surrounding "soulless" nature. This process of the gradual descent of the "I" took place during the cultural epochs of several thousands of years preceding the coming of Christ.

In ancient Greek culture, people still had a strong, albeit unconscious, memory of the pre-intellectual phase of culture, especially because it was exactly those Greeks who were the world pioneers in the definitive transition from the old to the new consciousness. This transition was prepared in the Greek temple mysteries; the great myths, spread by poets and bards, express this in the most diverse images. It was known that the rise of intellectuality, together with the descent of the "I," brought about a critical change not only in consciousness, but also in the earthly nature of humanity.

This earthly nature of human beings has three parts: the physical-material body, the complex of life forces also called life body or etheric body, and the soul body called astral body in spiritual science. In the last two cases, the word *body* should of course not be understood in a material sense. For an extensive description of these three aspects of human nature the reader is referred to Rudolf Steiner's book *Theosophy*.

The critical change (or metamorphosis), mentioned above, of the three aspects of earthly human nature, was a process of condensation. The original condition of the body with the life and soul processes working in it was much more pliant and more permeable to the spiritual than later. A certain hardening began to take place, with the result that human beings began to feel more independent and secure in themselves, but were at the same time cut off from the spiritual world. Due to this development they now observed out of their own consolidated nature an outside world in which they could no longer perceive any ensoulment by beings. The old clairvoyance was replaced by the intellect.

In this condensation process the Greeks still saw the work of a divine power, named *Hecate*. Hecate was a threefold goddess; she was portrayed with a *dagger* and a *serpent*, a *key* and *snares*, and a *torch*. These objects have symbolic meanings that have to be viewed in relation to the three "bodies" of the human being mentioned above.

The serpent and the dagger relate to the physical body. Because of the condensation process this body becomes more dependent on its physical environment for its health, which in prior ages had been more connected with cosmic-spiritual influences. The dagger is here the image of the influence of illness that can penetrate into the body from outside. The serpent is a symbol that we also find with Asclepius, the god of healing.

The key with snares and the torch have to do with knowledge. The torch of knowledge is lighted in the soul, but access, the key, to knowledge lies in reflection, which is the work of the etheric body. For we would never be able to make conscious the impressions from the world that we form in our psyche if the finer life processes in the brain did not fulfill this reflecting function. The etheric body had this function already in the pre-intellectual, clairvoyant consciousness; it made the "astral" images perceptible by its reflective capacity. The snares are the picture of the folds in the brain where the threads of thought have to be spun like the thread of Ariadne in the story of Theseus in the labyrinth of the Minotaur.

For modern people this may all sound fantastic and implausible, but that is because current scientific conceptions of the human being are very far removed from the mystery knowledge in ancient cultures. However, when we supplement the current natural scientific picture of the human being, which is impressive but one-sided, with insights from modern "mystery" knowledge, the mythological pictures of ancient civilizations appear in a surprising light. Such a modern mystery knowledge is to be found in the work of Rudolf Steiner. The insights developed there make us realize that former knowledge of the human being, that was expressed in mythological pictures, exceeds our current knowledge in depth and greatness. The attributes of threefold Hecate turn out to be no childish fantasies, but strikingly accurate symbols for spiritual realities. Deep wonder and boundless respect fill us when in Shakespeare's work we find that he used mythological representations in a way that confirms the explanations of spiritual science.

Macbeth is a person in whose soul the transition from the old clairvoyance to the new intellectual consciousness proceeds abnormally. The Hecate force of change can work in a malicious way when the "I," in its egotism, cuts itself off from the higher world. That is why in antiquity already Hecate was viewed in the light of death and evil. The condensation of the three earthly sheaths of the "I" may be a good and necessary process, but it also contains a twofold danger. First, the old clairvoyant capacity becomes decadent. In the time of Christ and even centuries earlier, a demonization of this ancient capacity was taking place everywhere. People still tried to create a connection with "the gods" by orgiastic and black-magical rituals and practices. The formerly sacred mystery wisdom was abused for the purpose of exercising egotistical power. This is most evident with the later Egyptian pharaohs and the Roman Caesars.

The second danger proves to be part of the nature of the new capacity that replaces the former one. The young, awakening intellect runs the risk of immediately falling into cunning and cynicism. We see this in those Greek sophists who abused thinking to justify anything, and also in the Jewish Pharisees whose cold scholarship and cynical hypocrisy have become proverbial.

This early corruption of the still budding intellect could only be counteracted if the chilly brain was warmed by the power of love. For the Greeks this was the love of wisdom, philo-sophia. It developed virtues that guided the rapid unfolding of egoism into a beneficial direction for true ego development. The three "soul sisters," thinking, feeling, and the will, have to be nourished by the "I" with the forces of the three Platonic virtues, wisdom, courage and temperance. When this does not happen, then the "three weird sisters" raise their ugly heads, the bony witches as counter-images of these three soul forces, demonized by the Hecate-condensation of human nature.

In sagas and fairy tales, the fully conscious human "I" is often indicated by the image of the "new king." Destiny called Macbeth to this dignity, but he let himself be guided by vices. His murder of sleeping, defenseless people is the work of a coward; thoughtless and unwise is the way he violently seized the highest power. The witches speak the truth—also the shocking imaginations they show him in the cave in the fourth act contain truth—but Macbeth is incapable of interpreting these truths in the right way. The Hecate influence works to his disadvantage in his unstable, atavistic nature.

Is it a coincidence that in the murder scene of the second act the Hecate symbols appear? There is the vision of the *dagger*, the *key* with which the porter opens the gate, and the *torch* carried by the servant to light the way for Banquo and his son. We may assume that Shakespeare did not use these symbols intentionally. The deeper meaning of Hecate's influence was probably not something he knew in his waking day-consciousness. But from unconscious regions of his soul, the genius of the poet called forth precisely those words and images that manifest the spiritual reality of the dramatic situations.

The child with the Tree of Life

Where is the light to offset all this darkness? One of Shakespeare's foremost qualities is his noble morality. He has the ability to show, over against the deepest chasms of evil, the sunny heights of the good. Even more than for his impressive evocation of evil, we can admire him for his radiantly shining pictures of the highest and most noble human virtues.

Here also he never resorts to an allegorical or moralistic element. He shows the good by means of his lifelike characters and dramatic situations themselves. We realize then that he fathoms the good just as profoundly as evil. He must have had the deepest understanding of the true significance of the Christ mystery.

I have described the entire tragedy of Macbeth as a progressive disintegration of the essence of the human being by the threefold murder of the Father, the Fellow Human Being, and the Child. Through this dark forest of horrors that end with the death of Macbeth, runs a golden thread of light that leads to the ultimate redemption. This is the thread of the "true king." The picture of the true king appears three times in the drama: the wise Healer, the holy figure of Edward the Confessor who does not appear in person; then the son of Duncan, young Malcolm; and finally Fleance, the son of Banquo, the future ancestor of later generations of kings. In summary, however, we can say that the "true king" is represented imaginatively by "the Child."

Just as the royal Jesus child once had to flee from the destructive powers of the black magician Herod, here the royal "children," Malcolm and Fleance, also have to flee. Malcolm is no longer a child in the literal sense. He is a youth with a certain life experience: witness his quick judgment of the dangerous situation after the murder of his father and the way he tests Macduff in their conversation in England (4.3). But on the imaginative level he is certainly the child, the carrier of the triumphal power of the good.

Macduff, who in the final battle overcomes the tyrant and comes on the stage holding the latter's chopped-off head, also has to be viewed in relation to "the child." Not only because the "Herodian" children's murder is directed specifically against him, but also because the imaginative apparition in the witches' cave, which points to his decisive role in the drama, shows the image of a blood-covered child, in other words, a child that has been taken out of the womb by surgical intervention.

Here we touch on the mysterious visions that were shown to Macbeth in the witches' cave, and which form in a certain sense the key to understanding the whole drama. It is incomprehensible that among the commentators on Shakespeare's work there is uncertainty as to the significance of these visions.

What the witches show to Macbeth are all images of the future and warnings that in themselves contain nothing but truth. There is, however, an interesting difference between the *images* that are shown and the *words* that sound with them. The images: the helmeted head, the blood-covered child, and the crowned child holding a tree in its hand, are true, but hard to interpret. The words, by contrast: "Macbeth! Beware Macduff!"; "... none of woman born shall harm Macbeth"; "Macbeth shall never vanquished be until Great Birnam Wood to high Dunsinane hill shall come against him"— these words may be pretty clear in their meaning, but extremely misleading for him who does not understand the images. And indeed, Macbeth does not understand them and therefore draws the wrong conclusions.

He does not understand that the helmeted head is his own decapitated head; that the blood-covered child indicates the particular circumstance of Macduff's birth, because of which he is one not "of woman born" and therefore is in a position to kill Macbeth. And finally, he does not understand that the crowned child is Malcolm with a branch in his hand that he had cut from Birnam Wood. For Malcolm will order his troops to cut branches off the trees and approach behind this camouflage the castle of Dunsinane, where Macbeth is holed up. The lookout on the tower then sees a walking wood ascending the hill on which the castle stands. When he reports this to his lord, Macbeth understands that one of his safety factors is lost. It will soon become evident that the other prediction, on which he had based the second part of his security, has also misled him. He fancies himself invulnerable for weapons used against him by human hands, for no mortal is not "of woman born." And he failed to connect the first prediction ("Beware Macduff!") with this.

Macbeth wanted certainty from the witches regarding his destiny. By their sinister brew in the cauldron they are able to conjure up visions for his spiritual eye. But these visions deceive him because he has already violently broken his real connection with the wisdom of destiny by his murders of Duncan and Banquo.

It has already been pointed out that Shakespeare indicates this with the words: "Macbeth does murder sleep ... Macbeth shall sleep no more!" In the unconscious condition of sleep, human beings enter into a direct connection with their own higher being, the genius which, together with higher powers in the spiritual world, judges their deeds. In sleep the "balance sheet" of our lives is drawn up; the world of sleep is the world of the "weavers of destiny." Those who "murder sleep" cut their own bridge that connects them with the weavers of destiny. He ends up in the cave of the evil spinners of fate or brewers of a disgusting gruel that, like a kind of drug, brings on madness and estrangement.

Lady Macbeth is tormented by her conscience *in her sleep*; she who was a devil ends her life as a tragic human being. Macbeth, who initially still heard the voice of conscience, who is still tormented in *sleepless* nights by the horrors he commits, ends his life as a senselessly raging devil. The last violent act he commits is again directed at a child: he kills the young son of Siward, the general of the English army.

The third vision in the witches' cave has, however, a still deeper meaning than what has been mentioned so far. The crowned child holding a tree in its hand indicates a being that carries the Tree of Life. It is an imagination of the Savior who restores the Tree of Life that was withdrawn from humanity at the fall into sin.

What does the symbol of the Tree of Life mean? We can understand this best when we consider the first years of the life of a human child. Until children call themselves "I" they do not yet fully live as earthly beings. The fullness of the cosmic-spiritual world is then still working in them. It is not only the aftereffect of "heavenly" powers that have led the spiritual "I"-being to earthly birth, it is also the actual, active work of these powers through which small children are formed. A spiritual fullness of life is creatively active in the as-yet hardly conscious little beings who, in a condition of paradisal innocence, pass through their first and all-important phase of becoming human. This creative fullness of life is indicated with the symbol or imagination of the Tree of Life.

When we call a very little child "angelic," we mean this unearthly, innocent nature of the first phase of life. Spiritual science makes us realize that more is at work here than just something angelic. Before a first form of consciousness of self awakens, the child is still a carrier of the Tree of Life in which the fullness of the cosmic-spiritual worlds is concentrated.

Once upon a time, human beings lived continually in this paradisal state, but a change occurred by the influence of Lucifer. The development of consciousness was accelerated by this influence: human beings received a kind of surrogate "I," a distorted reflection of the true "I," and they obtained knowledge of the world. Their eyes were opened to the outer appearance of things; they became inhabitants of the earth in mortal, material bodies. Their knowledge of the earth and themselves was purchased at the price of death. In human beings the Tree of Life shriveled up and became the death Tree of Knowledge. The fullness of life was withdrawn from them; only in unconscious children and in sleep did the Tree of Life continue to bestow its beneficial forces on human beings.

But what was once lost can be regained. When the true "I," not the luciferic "I," is born, life can rise again out of death. Christ brings to earth the true "I." He enables human beings in their spiritless waking consciousness to achieve the resurrection of the living spirit. What still works *unconsciously* in sleep and in the little child, can begin to work *consciously* in the Christ-permeated "I": the Tree of Life is bestowed again on human beings who have now awakened to freedom. This is why Christ said to his disciples: "Truly, I say to you, whoever does not receive the Kingdom of God like a child shall not enter it" (Mk 10:15 RSV). It does not mean that adults have to become unconscious and innocent again like little children, but that they must now in consciousness become like children are in their unconsciousness: filled with the divine.

The "evil king," the luciferic "I," is vanquished by the "true king," the child holding the Tree of Life in its hand. Malcolm becomes the carrier of the power of the Healer because he has met the royal healer in England, who makes an army available to him to combat Macbeth. One could also say that he thus received the power to overcome evil.

Suicide and premature birth

To conclude this contemplation of *Macbeth,* I want to call attention to a remarkable motif which is not without importance in the composition of the play. It is the contrast between Lady Macbeth and Macduff, the *suicide* and the one *untimely born*. Suicide is an acceleration of death by one's own deed; untimely birth is in this case an acceleration of birth by the hand of another. In both cases we have to do with a deed that goes counter to nature, but the suicide occurs as the tragic end of a hopeless situation, while the premature birth is the beginning of a future power that turns evil to the good. Lady Macbeth's suicide has its origin in the past: her share in the murder of King Duncan, which opened the door to a whole series of horrific deeds. The "operative" birth of Macduff has its fulfillment in the future: only a man "not of woman born" will be able to vanquish Macbeth and thus put an end to the horrific deeds.

Lady Macbeth is childless. Maybe it is the sterility of her womb that has hardened this woman and made her insensible and unwomanly, causing her to become an instigator of evil. Macduff is made childless by the murderous terror of Macbeth. His hard masculinity melts for a moment under the overwhelming feelings that assail him when he hears of the death of his entire family. He says:

> O, I could play the woman with mine eye,
> And braggart with my tongue. But, gentle heavens,
> Cut short all intermission. [4.3]

He pulls himself together, and, from that moment, guided by the spirits of his murdered wife and children, strives for the annihilation of the evil personified in Macbeth.

By working the polarity between untimely birth and suicide into his tragedy, Shakespeare connects the motif of evil with the motif of birth and death. In every cultural epoch in history we always see one of the great riddles of life taking center stage in human thinking and experience. In our time, the so-called New Age that began with the Renaissance and will stretch over many centuries into the future, the central riddle of life is the mystery of evil. Human consciousness is being confronted with this in our time. The history of the twentieth century makes this abundantly clear. In science and politics, everywhere in society at large, we see evil entering into action in different guises. Political and "private" criminality is just one of its visible symptoms. Most of humanity is still too much caught up in materialism to see through evil as a spiritual, but also concrete power. For the future, however, it may be expected that spiritual-scientific insights will break through in this regard.

In a previous epoch the central riddle of life was the mystery of birth and death. For the Christian culture of Europe this was focused on the riddle of the birth and death of Jesus of Nazareth. How the *divine* worked in this *human* birth and death became the great question of faith. This was expressed in the images of the Virgin with the Child and of the Crucifix, images which dominated the minds of people for centuries. In this regard it is significant that Shakespeare in his tragedy *Macbeth*, in which he dramatically shows the transition from an old to a new era, has woven together these two mysteries of life—evil as well as birth and death.

Suicide, the self-willed acceleration of death, brings it about that after death the soul maintains a very strong connection with the abruptly terminated earthly life. There is an essential difference between suicide and premature death due to illness or accident in which destiny plays a role. Although the deed of suicide is most frequently the result of a dimming of consciousness, and therefore a deed for which a person cannot be held wholly accountable, the force that is directed against one's own life must still be considered as a willful violation of one's own destiny. It has weighty consequences in the life after death.

The Christian Church—originally probably on the basis of spiritual insight, later purely by tradition—has stigmatized suicide as an unpardonable sin. An age in which the belief in eternal hell has virtually totally disappeared, and justifiably so, calls for a new spiritual insight concerning the consequences of suicide.

After the moment of death, the individual human spirit passes through a period of catharsis before it is able to ascend into a higher spiritual existence. The "place of catharsis," in Indian tradition called *Kamaloka*, is described in modern spiritual science as a condition in which everything that binds the deceased to their earthly existence has to be dissolved: all desire, passion, wishes, in brief, all egoistic tendencies. In addition, everything of which the deceased have become guilty during their life on earth vis-à-vis others as well as themselves, has to be reviewed and worked through so that, on the one hand, the individual spirits do not remain "contaminated" by this on their further journey through higher worlds. On the other hand, an awareness of a "debt owed" arises and is preserved as an important part of the destiny of the individual's next life, that can be taken up again at their new birth. This Kamaloka condition, in which the impure, lower nature of human beings has to be dissolved and purified, is a painful death process, especially for those who, during their life on earth, have let themselves be guided by their egoism.

When destiny itself has led human beings to an early death, the purification process is completely different from the case of suicide. In the latter case there will be so many unfulfilled desires in the soul that post-mortal consciousness will be overwhelmed by torments of the soul. This has consequences for the next earthly life.

Dante gives us a moving picture in the thirteenth canto of his *Inferno* of the penalties suffered by suicides.

The souls have been changed into bushes and trees—plants therefore, but endowed with feeling. Evil harpies eat their leaves causing them the most intense pain. The picture of plants indicates a dimming of consciousness that is the consequence of suicide. Suicides are unable to let go of the earthly; their consciousness is burdened with the past, and therefore it is dimmed for new spiritual conditions after death.

In the case of premature birth this is exactly the reverse: the time when the spiritual individuality enters the world with the body that was formed in the mother's womb is not yet ripe. The consequence of this is that such people, in a certain sense, show a tendency in their lives to float above themselves a little, so that they don't stand squarely in earthly life. At the same time, however, such people are often endowed with a sensitivity for the future. It is known that the Apostle Paul was such a prematurely born person.

We may ask what the cause of such sensitivity for the future in a prematurely born person might be. It is a question that cannot be answered with a few words. Maybe it becomes somewhat understandable if we remember that the entire future lies fully prepared in the hands of the spiritual world which, by the way, does not contradict human freedom. After all, the intentions the gods have for us must be brought to realization on earth by us, human beings. A spiritual impulse may or may not be followed by human beings; every individual is free to work with it or pass it by. When one human being does not follow such an impulse, the divine world has to wait for someone else to do it.

People who at the moment of their birth are not quite fully "ready" for the earth, carry in themselves a feeling for future potential because they are still a little bit more "heavenly" than full-term children. Macduff is not "of woman born." That does not need to mean that he was a seven month baby, but at any rate he is, according to his own words, "from his mother's womb untimely ripp'd," prematurely pulled from the womb. His being is focused on the future in the same way that Lady Macbeth is tormented by the past.

Thus with the death of Lady Macbeth and the birth of Macduff, Shakespeare indicates the mystery of death as such. He turns us, without didactic emphasis, to the life after death and the life before birth. He does not say anything particular about it; he evokes questions in us. His dramatic dreams are laden with the deepest mysteries of humanity as well as divinity.

"Life's but a walking shadow" when human beings between birth and death do not find the power of their divine origin which transcends the limits of birth and death.

4

HAMLET

—

Tragedy of Materialism

Poisoning and death

In our contemplations of *The Merchant of Venice, A Midsummer Night's Dream,* and *Macbeth,* we have seen that at the beginning of the last act Shakespeare gives us a key for opening the deeper meaning of the drama. In *Hamlet, Prince of Denmark* this is also the case.

Act V begins with the famous scene in the churchyard of Elsinore where Hamlet and his friend Horatio are watching a grave-digger prepare a grave from which he throws out half-decomposed bones of old corpses while digging a pit for one newly deceased. In a comically sinister conversation between Hamlet, the grave-digger, and Horatio, in which the latter, true to his "Watson" role, just says "yes sir," Hamlet unfolds his thoughts of the "low destiny" of the human being: death is the irrevocable end; human beings pass away and return to *dust.*

Immediately after this comes the nocturnal procession that accompanies the remains of the fair Ophelia to the grave. Wrestling with Ophelia's brother Laertes in the open grave, Hamlet cries out his love for the unfortunate girl. He wants to fight Laertes in a duel "upon this theme."

This takes place in the last scene. But what was meant by Hamlet to be a chivalrous fight ends up in murder by the foul play of the king. Dying of the poison on Laertes' foil, Hamlet is still able to use this weapon to carry out the repeatedly postponed revenge on his uncle, the king. Laertes too is wounded by the poisoned point of the foil, because at one moment during the duel the foils were accidentally exchanged. Unknowingly, Hamlet's mother drinks from the cup of poisoned wine which the king had intended for his nephew, in case he would not be hit by Laertes' foil.

Thus the end of the tragedy presents us, four times, with *death by poison*. This ending can be viewed as the consequence of the dramatic process that unfolds throughout the tragedy, the consequence of the personalities of the principal characters; however, here too it is possible, as in other plays, to fathom the *imaginative* significance of the ending.

At the level of imagination, the horrific poisonings at the end are the consequences of Hamlet's philosophy, which is most clearly expressed in the scene with the gravedigger. This philosophy is none other than *materialism*. Materialism knows death only as a turning to dust. That the immortal soul rises out of the death of matter is something that in this worldview is denied. The only reality materialism knows is matter; the reality, in other words, of what is dead.

When thinking denies the spirit, human deeds lead to poisoning and death. This could be the quintessence of the tragedy of Hamlet when we summarize in words what the dramatic pictures express at the level of imagination.

Does not the twentieth century provide us with proof of this thesis? Aren't we seeing around us the consequences of what was beginning in Shakespeare's time: the dominance of materialism in western culture? Are not poisoning and death, in the end, the only possible results of materialistic thinking? Think of gas chambers, chemical weapons, air, water, and earth pollution by dead chemical substances—to mention just the most obvious examples. What the tragedy of *Hamlet* still shows in *images* became reality long ago.

When using the words *materialism* or *materialist*, we should let go of a connotation that has grown over time in day-to-day usage. Calling a person a materialist today calls up an image of someone who is only interested in sensory pleasures, a money-grubber, obsessed with the acquisition of worldly possessions. Of course that does not apply at all to Hamlet. Materialism as a world view has the most noble representatives, and among those Hamlet is in a certain sense the first one. Nevertheless, the consequences of a certain way of thinking can lead to the opposite of what its proponents proclaim, witness the convincing examples of some atomic scientists.

One can make the objection that it is not Hamlet who sets up the perfidious poisoning but Laertes who was enmeshed in the intrigues of Hamlet's uncle. Such an objection would merely prove that the three levels, which I have now often mentioned, are being confused. In the outer realistic and inner psychological development of the drama we see of course that Laertes in his lust for revenge, and the king in his perfidiousness, concoct the poison plan; at the imaginative, irrational level, however, the relationships are different.

To make this clear I have to relate the whole tragedy in brief. Then we will attempt to recognize the dramatic dream pictures as spiritual realities, following the same method as heretofore applied.

The story

Act I

The sentinels of the royal castle of Elsinore have seen the ghostly apparition of the recently deceased King

Hamlet during the night. At their request, Horatio, a fellow student of Prince Hamlet joins them on their watch. The ghost appears twice, but, in spite of Horatio's urging, it disappears without speaking a word. Horatio decides to report to Hamlet what they have seen.

In the castle the new king speaks about his deceased brother and of his marriage with the latter's widow. He then mentions the aggressive plans of the Norwegian Prince Fortinbras. He sends two emissaries to Norway to negotiate.

Laertes, the son of Polonius, a councilor of the king, asks for permission to return to France, from which he had come to Denmark for the coronation celebrations. He receives permission.

Prince Hamlet gives clear evidence of his grief for the loss of his father. His mother and uncle try to comfort him and reproach him at the same time for his all too emphatic show of mourning. His request to return to Wittenberg where he was studying is not granted. Left alone, Hamlet gives vent to his feelings. He speaks the most bitter words about the remarriage of his mother less than two months after the death of her noble king, a marriage with a good-for-nothing compared with the old Hamlet.

Horatio enters and reports the apparition of the ghost of the deceased king. Hamlet is deeply touched by this news. They agree to join the watch that same night.

In Polonius's house Laertes says goodbye to his sister Ophelia and urges her not to take Hamlet's declarations of love seriously, because the distance between a prince and the daughter of a councilor is too great. When Laertes has left, Polonius asks Ophelia what brother and sister had been talking about. In turn, he too underlines Laertes' warning and he orders his daughter to limit her contact with Hamlet to the minimum.

During the night watch the specter appears. It motions Hamlet to a sequestered spot and tells him there the story of his death. While asleep in the garden he was murdered by his brother who had poured poison in his ear. The poor ghost who, unredeemed, has to wander and is tormented in purgatory exhorts his son to revenge him on the murderer. The guilty mother, however, who had been seduced by the villainous brother-in-law, must not be injured.

Hamlet wants to dedicate himself entirely to the commandment of the ghost; everything else is to be purged from his memory. At his writing table he writes down the crime of his uncle. Horatio and Marcellus have to swear that they won't tell anyone what they have seen, and also will not show that they know anything special about him if Hamlet should start acting strangely.

Act II

Polonius sends a man to Paris to spy on Laertes there. Ophelia reports the strange behavior of Hamlet who came to see her in a doleful condition. Without speaking to her he looked at her with pain and grief in his eyes. Polonius interprets this behavior as bewildered infatuation and leaves to report it to the king.

The king has called for Rosencrantz and Guildenstern to cheer up their friend Hamlet whose condition is, day by day, becoming more alarming. The emissaries to Norway return with favorable news. Young Fortinbras will not use his troops against Denmark but against Poland. He is asking for free passage through Denmark.

Polonius tells the king that, in his opinion, Hamlet is crazy with love. He proposes to send his daughter to Hamlet; the king can then overhear their conversation and convince himself of the amorous madness of his nephew.

Hamlet enters and Polonius addresses him. Hamlet

plays the part of a fool and indeed, he fools Polonius. Rosencrantz and Guildenstern come in to talk with Hamlet, but the latter immediately sees through their intentions.

A group of actors appears, and Hamlet lets the first one show him his art: the story of the murder of King Priam of Troy. When the troupe has left Hamlet takes stock of himself. He curses his weakness, his inability to execute the revenge. He wants to let the actors perform something for his uncle which, because of its similarity to his own crime, will shake him so badly that his reaction betrays him. Hamlet considers such proof necessary because the apparition of the ghost could have been a devil that wants to destroy him. The play is to set a trap for the conscience of his uncle.

Act III

Rosencrantz and Guildenstern report on their fruitless efforts to discover the cause of Hamlet's depression and madness. They do mention that the arrival of the actors cheered him up a bit. In Hamlet's name, Polonius invites the king and queen to attend the evening performance.

Ophelia has been told to talk to Hamlet so that her father and the king can eavesdrop on the conversation and gain an impression of Hamlet's condition.

Hamlet enters and speaks of death. He thinks that all who are weighed down by the unbearable burden of life would make an end of it, were it not that fear of the unknown after death dissuades them from it. Reflection, consciousness make cowards of us all; they lame our decisiveness.

In the conversation with Ophelia, which follows, Hamlet's words are a poignant mixture of feigned madness, dissembled love, and genuine despair. Ophelia is profoundly shocked by what she hears and sees.

In the king's opinion, love is not the cause of Hamlet's

condition. He fears a dangerous outburst and decides to send him to England for his diversion and, who knows, cure. Polonius insists that Hamlet is mad with love and proposes that the queen have a talk with him. He will secretly eavesdrop on the conversation. Should she be unable to coax anything out of Hamlet, let him then be sent to England or be locked up.

The actors receive their instructions from Hamlet who also asks Horatio to keenly observe the king. Then the play begins in the presence of the king, the queen, and the court. Preceded by a pantomime which briefly summarizes the action, it shows events that took place in Denmark: a queen attests to her love for her spouse; the latter falls asleep and his malevolent cousin drops poison into his ear. (The pantomime had already shown that the murderer then succeeds in winning the queen.)

Hamlet's uncle is terribly upset and runs out of the room; everyone else follows in consternation, except Hamlet and Horatio. Proof of the king's guilt has been clearly shown. Rosencrantz and Guildenstern arrive with the message that the queen wants to speak to her son.

The king is deeply conscious of his crime. He bitterly blames himself and falls on his knees to pray. On his way to his mother's apartment, Hamlet sees the king on his knees. He already pulls his sword, but then reflects that he does not want to kill him with his soul purified. He postpones the deed to a moment when the king's soul will certainly be doomed.

Hamlet's conversation with the queen begins so vehemently that Polonius behind his curtain calls for help. Hamlet, thinking it is the king, thrusts his sword through the curtain and kills the old man.

Hamlet now sharply reproaches his mother for her hasty marriage to the king; his words touch her deeply. The ghost of the old king appears and urges Hamlet once again to revenge, but also calls for compassion on his mother. The queen thinks Hamlet is completely mad when he speaks to the ghost, because she is not able to see it. Hamlet forcefully declares that he is not mad at all. He warns his mother not to share the bed of his uncle in the coming night and to tell him nothing of their conversation. He leaves her, dragging the dead Polonius behind him.

Act IV

The queen tells the king that Hamlet has killed Polonius in a fit of madness. Hamlet now has to be sent to England immediately. His companions, Rosencrantz and Guildenstern, receive sealed orders that upon arrival in England Hamlet has to be killed. On his way to the ship, Hamlet meets the passing army of Fortinbras. He compares the impetuous activity of the Norwegian with his own incapacity to come to a deed.

At the court in Elsinore, the king and queen are wit-nessing an agonizing scene: Ophelia has lost her mind due to the death of her father and the perceived ruin of Hamlet's spirit. Singing songs and speaking con-fused words she wanders about. Laertes, returned from France, comes raging into the castle, followed by a muti-nous mob. He demands revenge for the death of his father. The king manages to quiet him down and prom-ises a judicial investigation. Ophelia comes in again and Laertes has to witness how the insane girl goes about mumbling and singing and handing little flowers to people.

Horatio receives a letter from Hamlet. In a struggle with pirates at sea Hamlet jumped onto the pirates' ship. He was well treated there and is now back in Denmark. The sailors who bring this letter also have one for the king.

The king has succeeded in convincing Laertes that

Hamlet is the only guilty one. A messenger brings Hamlet's letter with the news that he is back in Denmark. Now the king and Laertes prepare a plan for his death. By challenging Hamlet to a fencing duel Laertes will be able to kill him. He will take a sharp foil and poison its point. At that moment the queen comes in with the message that Ophelia has drowned.

Act V

Two gravediggers are working in a cemetery. The grave they are digging is, they say, for someone who has committed suicide. The first gravedigger sends the second one away to get a pint and, singing, continues his work. Hamlet and Horatio arrive and philosophize together about the bones that are thrown out of the new grave. Hamlet addresses the gravedigger who then shows him the skull of a certain Yorick, the jester of the old king.

Hamlet picks up the skull and speaks to it as if it were the last, stinking remains of his beloved Yorick. Human beings, he says, face a lowly fate: they completely decay to dust. A funeral procession enters with the king, the queen, and courtiers. The priest wants to make it brief, because the death of the deceased was suspicious. Laertes jumps into the grave of his sister. He curses Hamlet whose deed caused Ophelia's death. Hamlet now appears and wrestles with Laertes in the open grave. He openly declares his love for Ophelia. He wants a duel with Laertes.

Hamlet tells Horatio of his adventures during the sea voyage. He secretly opened the sealed orders and read his own death sentence. He then wrote a different order saying that Rosencrantz and Guildenstern had to be killed upon arrival.

Before the duel takes place Hamlet reconciles himself with Laertes. He says that his madness made him do things that did not come from his true inner being.

Laertes accepts the apology but does not want to give up the duel. The foils are brought; the fight begins. After the first hit the king wants to let Hamlet drink some wine from a cup into which he had thrown a pearl, but Hamlet first wants to fence some more. The queen takes the cup and drinks. The warning from the king, who had poisoned the wine, comes too late. Laertes wounds Hamlet with the poisoned foil. In a struggle they exchange foils without noticing it, and now Laertes is wounded.

The queen dies. Laertes falls and confesses the traitorous plot: Hamlet is doomed to die of the poison in his wound. Hearing that, Hamlet thrusts the poisonous foil into the body of his uncle, the king. He also pours the rest of the poisoned wine into the king's mouth.

Laertes asks Hamlet to forgive him as he had forgiven Hamlet; then he dies. Hamlet asks his friend Horatio to make known to the world what has really taken place. Dying, he gives his vote to young Fortinbras as successor to the throne. The latter walks on stage triumphant from his victory over the Polish army. He accepts the crown of Denmark and orders a full state funeral for Hamlet.

The limits of consciousness

No other play by Shakespeare has been the subject of so many opinions, reviews, and commentaries as *Hamlet*. Ever since it was written it has captivated theater audiences and readers alike and evoked questions in them. It has been criticized for its involved, incoherent composition, and for its melodramatic ending with four dead bodies on the stage. It has been admired for its greatness and profundity. But no matter what opinion one has of the play and its leading part, Hamlet has always been viewed as the most human, truly the most complete and genuine human being in the whole realm of humanity that Shakespeare created in his theater works. About Hamlet we know more than about Shakespeare himself.

In Hamlet human beings of modern times recognize themselves much more readily than, for instance, in the figure of Faust whom, if possible, Goethe actually sketched as an even more complete and true representative of modern times. The reason for this will become evident in the course of this study. First we want to consider the question of whether there is a relationship between Hamlet and Faust, when they are both called representatives of our time.

Hamlet was studying at Wittenberg, the university where Professor Faust taught. Why couldn't we imagine Hamlet listening to the brilliant, somewhat cynical lectures of the famous doctor? Those were the lectures in which for ten years he "led his students by the nose" while he knew "that we can know nothing." Couldn't it have been Faust who sowed the seed of doubt, of agnosticism into the soul of the young prince? Was Goethe perhaps keenly aware of the connection between Hamlet and Faust?

In Goethe's novel *Wilhelm Meister* we see how Wilhelm, who, like Faust, shares many traits with Goethe himself, immerses himself intensely into the drama and figure of Hamlet. The traveling actors to which he belongs give a Hamlet performance in a modified form—a Wilhelmian (read: Goethean) form in which the study in Wittenberg is scratched out. Let us further remember that Goethe wrote his poem *Bei Betrachtung von Schillers Schädel** as a kind of answer to Hamlet's contemplation of Yorick's skull, and, finally, how in the scene of Faust's interment the Lemurians sing the same song that the gravedigger in

---

* *In Contemplation of Schiller's Skull.*

the cemetery of Elsinore sings. It is evident that Goethe was conscious of the relationship between Hamlet and Faust, at least to the extent that these two figures had great significance for him, and that he recognized both the Hamlet problem and the Faust problem in his own development. What then is really the Hamlet problem?

In the current epoch, which began with the Renaissance and the Reformation, every human being who wrestles with existential questions of what it means to be human runs up against Hamlet. Every human being lives with the Hamlet problem in the soul, the problem of the *limits of consciousness*.

> To be, or not to be, that is the question:
> Whether 'tis nobler in the mind to suffer
> The slings and arrows of outrageous fortune,
> Or to take arms against a sea of troubles,
> And by opposing end them. To die, to sleep,
> No more; and by a sleep to say we end
> The heart-ache and the thousand natural shocks
> That flesh is heir to—'tis a consummation
> Devoutly to be wish'd. To die, to sleep;
> To sleep! Perchance to dream—ay, there's the rub;
> For in that sleep of death what dreams may come,
> When we have shuffled off this mortal coil,
> Must give us pause: there's the respect
> That makes calamity of so long life;
> For who would bear the whips and scorns of time,
> Th' oppressor's wrong, the proud man's contumely,
> The pangs of despis'd love, the law's delay,
> The insolence of office, and the spurns
> That patient merit of the unworthy takes,
> When he himself might his quietus make
> With a bare bodkin? who would fardels bear,
> To grunt and sweat under a weary life,
> But that the dread of something after death—

The undiscover'd country from whose bourn
No traveler returns—puzzles the will,
And makes us rather bear those ills we have
Than fly to others that we know not of?
Thus conscience does make cowards of us all;
And thus the native hue of resolution
Is sicklied o'er with the pale cast of thought;
And enterprises of great pitch and moment,
With this regard, their currents turn awry,
And lose the name of action.... [3.1]

The great German philosopher Eduard von Hartmann (1842-1906) came to the conclusion that collective suicide was the only plausible solution to the fundamental problem of being human, the problem that lies in the misery of existence itself. But, he said, the animals would not organize such a general suicide day, and eventually new human beings would develop again out of the animals. Therefore, it would be better to focus all human intellect on the development of a machine with which one can drill to a great depth into the earth and then use an extraordinarily strong explosive to blow the whole earth apart. That was supposed to be the right ultimate aim.

Where did Hartmann's profound pessimism come from? It came from the same worldview that underlies Hamlet's pessimism, namely the idea that human beings no longer remember the deeper ground of being, that which gives meaning to human life and also gives meaning to all pain, to "the slings and arrows of outrageous fortune." "To be, or not to be, that is the question." But this antithesis already includes the prejudice that to be turns into not to be when it ceases to be as earthly-material existence. The dying Hamlet says to Horatio that he should tell the truth regarding the events that have taken place on earth—"the rest is silence." No word about the spiritual side of being!

Beginning with Shakespeare's contemporary Francis Bacon, and later especially under the influence of Immanuel Kant, the philosophy of modern times has developed in such a way that the spiritual aspect of the world was placed outside the limits of our consciousness. In his *Philosophy of the Unconscious* Eduard von Hartmann also accepts the prejudice of Kant that we cannot know anything about the world but our own representations of it which we lay over the world like a veil. From Schopenhauer, however, Hartmann adopted the idea that the "thing itself," i.e. the true reality of the world that is unknowable, is endowed with *will*. But, in the opinion of these philosophers, the will has no intelligence; only our representations have intelligence. Because the world is essentially determined by the stupidity of blind will, the world is bad. Reflecting on this we could raise the question of whether the cause of pessimism doesn't always lie in the creation of a boundary between the knowable and the unknowable.

Faust also comes to the idea of suicide by the painful experience of the limits of his consciousness:

> And see, that nothing can be known!
> *That* knowledge cuts me to the bone
>
> ...
>
> No dog would endure such a curst existence!*

Many people think that Hamlet's pessimism is caused by the shock of his father's death and the overhasty second marriage of his mother. But profoundly moving life experiences like this only lead to such depths of dejection when the soul is already diseased:

---

* J. W. von Goethe, *Faust A Tragedy*, Part I, tr. Bayard Taylor, The Modern Library, New York, 1950.

> ... the native hue of resolution
> Is sicklied o'er with the pale cast of thought...

It may be a psychological question how the change in Hamlet's behavior can be explained. For was he not an active, sportsmanlike young man, noble, idealistic, full of *savoir vivre* and of an exemplary princely bearing?

> The courtier's, soldier's, scholar's, eye, tongue, sword;
> Th' expectancy and rose of the fair state,
> The glass of fashion and the mold of form,
> Th' observed of all observers... [3.1]

Not a melancholy worrier who can only speak powerless words and never comes to a deed!

Here again, however, the psychological level, no matter how interesting, is secondary to the imaginative level. In *Hamlet* Shakespeare shows us, even more sharply drawn than in *Macbeth*, which was written later, and more clearly than in his dramas about kings, the transition from an old state of consciousness to a new—the transition from the Middle Ages to modern times.

Whether this transition is psychologically made fully plausible is not important; the imaginative character of the dramatic situation is overwhelmingly true. In order to bring this picture character to expression in full force, Shakespeare does not shrink from ignoring logical relationships. For, strictly speaking, it is not logical that someone who has just met the ghost of his deceased father, who told him of the terrors of an unredeemed soul existence after death, then says that death is "undiscover'd country from whose bourn no traveler returns," and that this person later says that the human being decays to dust: "Alexander died, Alexander was buried, Alexander returneth to dust; the dust is the earth. Of earth we make loam, and why of that loam, whereto he was converted, might they not stop a beer-barrel?" (5.1)

In Hamlet's soul we see a change that has transformed him from a fully engaged son of a king to a dejected outsider:

> I have of late—but wherefore I know not—lost all my mirth, forgone all custom of exercises; and indeed it goes so heavily with my disposition that this goodly frame, the earth, seems to me a sterile promontory; this most excellent canopy, the air, look you, this brave o'erhanging firmament, this majestical roof fretted with golden fire, why, it appears nothing to me but a foul and pestilent congregation of vapours. What a piece of work is man! How noble in reason! How infinite in faculties! In form and moving, how express and admirable! In action how like an angel! In apprehension how like a god! The beauty of the world, the paragon of animals. And yet to me what is this quintessence of dust? [2.2]

These words, spoken to Rosencrantz and Guildenstern, express Hamlet's condition: the world and the human being have lost all luster for him; they merely show themselves in their physical-material aspect. The earth is "a sterile promontory" covered with a "pestilent congregation of vapors," and in it lives the human being as an equally sad pile of dust.

In such a world Hamlet now stands as a spectator, critically and cynically observing with a superior intellect, but sick in his soul and powerless vis-à-vis reality. He feels this powerlessness as cowardice: "thus conscience does make cowards of us all," but the course of events shows that this sickness of the soul is worse than cowardice. It works destructively; it leads to death and ruin.

Seven innocent deaths are the result of Hamlet's state of consciousness: Polonius, Ophelia, Rosencrantz, Guildenstern, Laertes, the queen (not entirely innocent) and Hamlet himself. The dramatic imagery tells a clear story: death is the consequence of the change of consciousness undergone by Hamlet. Death is the reality to which actions lead that proceed from this changed consciousness. We need to take a closer look at this change in consciousness.

Being a spectator

It has struck a number of commentators of *Hamlet* that in no other Shakespeare play do the characters of the drama observe and spy and eavesdrop on each other as frequently as here. It seems to have been the intention of the poet to put particular emphasis on the motif of observation. This motif is introduced in the very first scene: the appearance of the ghost on the battlements of the royal castle is at first only observed. Even an insignificant episode like the first scene in Act II, when Polonius gives orders to a certain Reynaldo to watch what Laertes is doing in Paris—again, to observe— thus makes sense in the dramatic-imaginative totality of the play. It is as if Shakespeare wove a thread of *being a spectator* through the whole tragedy of *Hamlet*. This culminates in the third act in which the public watches Hamlet, Hamlet watches the king, and the king watches the play in the play.

Not only do the dramatic situations constantly accentuate the state of spectator consciousness, but Hamlet himself speaks out of this condition; he personifies, as it were, this spectator consciousness. The transformation of the soul constitution, which was mentioned in the previous section, is the transition from the medieval world of experience to the experience of the modern human being. Since the seventeenth century the western human being has become an observer, a spectator of the world.

Modern human beings are so accustomed to the soul

attitude of being a spectator that they can hardly imagine a different form of consciousness. We perceive the world out of an observation post. We climb into the tower of our head and from there we look about and form representations and concepts that have to explain the world that surrounds us.

In the process, we hardly notice that the world picture we thus conceive is determined by the form in which concepts arise in our consciousness. We think we can fathom reality by putting ourselves outside of reality. But what we actually do is form dead abstractions, mirror images of the world that do not come close to the deeper core of reality. The only realm that we can understand in this way, at least to some extent, is that of dead matter, where the forces of mechanics are at work.

Modern consciousness, which is the basis of our abstract, mechanistic concepts is bound to the nerve substance of our brain. This substance is virtually dead, and the working of our nerve-sense system involves a continual minimal death process, a breaking down, of which we become clearly aware after strenuous work, especially after nerve-wracking cerebral work. We perceive the death-bearing aspects of the world through our death-bearing organs: only like can know like.

But it is a fact that in this death process of consciousness human beings experience a remarkable strengthening of their individual self. Spectator consciousness is in essence nothing but a complete awakening of the human "I" to the physical-sensory world. This human condition only developed with the beginning of modern times. Previously, in the Middle Ages and in antiquity, consciousness had been different. Of course, the change had been prepared for a long time, but in the sixteenth and seventeenth centuries this development made a leap forward: the death-bearing element forcefully breaks through. Shakespeare lived precisely in the time period when this took place.

The different characteristic of the previous consciousness comes to expression in the fact that people still experienced the world as a meaningful, connected totality in which spiritual powers had an ordering role. The movements of the heavenly bodies, for instance, were considered to be the work of higher beings. Lorenzo in *The Merchant of Venice* still speaks of a heaven in which singing cherubim live in the movements of the stars.

It was the same with earthly nature, with the human being as the "crown of creation," and with the social order. Everything was still experienced as permeated by a spiritual-divine principle and ordered hierarchically in the form of a pyramid. In all realms of nature, including the human kingdom, "correspondences" were recognized, relationships with symbolic meanings. However, this symbolism was no intellectual game, but truth veiled in a picture. The grand relationship that was perceived was that of the great ordering in heaven above, the macrocosm, and the little ordering of the world below, the microcosm of the human being. These convictions regarding the reality of the world had become tradition in the Middle Ages, aftereffects of a state of consciousness in which the spiritual aspect of the world could still be directly experienced.

At one time, long ago, all of humanity possessed an original, dream-like clairvoyance that enabled them to enter into contact with spiritual beings of higher and lower ranks. All mythologies, sagas, fairy tales, and legends represent memories of this ancient state of consciousness. In the course of time this clairvoyant capacity dimmed and was replaced by sharp sense observation in conjunction with which intellectual thinking—brain thinking—also began to develop.

We can follow this process of the dimming of consciousness, the Twilight of the Gods, from the Egyptian-Babylonian culture into Greek and Roman times. While the ancient Greek had indeed become an intellectual, he/she still possessed an artistic imagination as a remnant of the old clairvoyance. The Roman, more or less lacking imagination, had already come very close to our modern rational consciousness. With the arrival of Christianity this trend toward intellectualization is at first slowed down—the power of faith opened human beings to the suprasensible again. Then, with modern times, this radically changed: the masterly beginning of this change is the new world picture of Copernicus. Heaven became an object of calculation, the earth a speck of dust in an immeasurable universe, and the human being a puny microbe that scratches about on this little piece of dust.

The old consciousness, that once existed in all peoples but did not simultaneously disappear in all of them, can be called *pre-reflective* consciousness. It was governed by those who cultivated the connection with "the realm of the gods" most strongly: the priests, the mages, the initiated kings. It is evident that these governors of this slowly disappearing state of consciousness were able to preserve their atavistic capacities best by maintaining a close *community through blood relationships*. The Egyptian Pharaoh married his sister; the priest castes were closely bound together through blood relationships. The Israelites, in whom just this reflective consciousness was already much more strongly developed than in the peoples around them, were forbidden to marry women from these peoples because through the bloodline the pre-reflective, clairvoyant consciousness would emerge again in the offspring from such unions.

The old consciousness, therefore, was connected with the blood. Love between a woman and a man had to remain within the connection through the blood in order to maintain this old consciousness. The death of a next of kin demanded revenge on the part of the relatives. The spirits of the deceased did not find rest until their blood was avenged by the surviving carriers of this blood. And these living relatives perceived the presence of the deceased; they experienced them in their dreams or in other ways.

The practice of blood feuds, in spite of the way they affect us now as primitive and horrible, once had their justified "morality" that was connected with the pre-reflective consciousness. Revenge of the murdered blood relative was the necessary counterpart of the love that was still tied to one's own blood.

In the tragedy of Hamlet we therefore see the pre-reflective consciousness represented by the impulse of blood revenge connected with the supernatural apparition of the murdered father. In a part of Hamlet's inner being this finds immediate resonance: he is ready and willing to avenge the death of his father. But his will is already lamed: he speaks of "the book and volume of my brain" in which he will imprint his intent of revenge, and then he writes it down; he makes a note for himself: "So, uncle, there you are."

But the will does not live in the brain! This is a psychological truth which modern human beings might learn from the tragedy of Hamlet. How differently does Orestes react when he is told by Apollo to avenge the murder of his father Agamemnon! Orestes acts immediately; he has no need of making notes in a little book. He kills Clytemnestra, his own mother. His will is strengthened by the love between brother and sister that connects him with Electra.

Hamlet, on the other hand, continually postpones the deed on the basis of deliberation. He breaks his connection with his beloved Ophelia—a significant fact in this context. The blood revenge he has to fulfill is thwarted by his love for a girl of lower standing that is completely outside any blood relationships. Thus the two states of consciousness, the old and the new, are both concurrently present in him. This makes him a tragically split person. Because of this, his pretended madness borders on real madness. Only, he does not lose his intelligence, but poor Ophelia does.

After his deed, Orestes has to undergo the torment of the Erinyes, the goddesses of revenge. In the drama written by Aeschylus he still sees the evil consequences of his matricide outside himself, clairvoyantly. In the tragedy by Euripides, who lived later, and who returned to the same theme, Orestes is no longer clairvoyant; he feels inwardly the voice of *conscience* that torments him. Within a century the transition was accomplished from a consciousness in which human beings *saw* spiritual images outside themselves to an inner imageless *knowing* of good and evil. The objection can be made that Aeschylus himself no longer possessed the old picture consciousness. That is undoubtedly correct, but he still possessed a living memory of it as a reality in his soul, while Euripides no longer felt this.

The words *conscience* and *consciousness* are closely related. Before the deed, Hamlet is tormented by conscience; and by the laming of his will caused by consciousness he also kills his mother, albeit indirectly. For her draught from the poisoned cup is the consequence of his postponement of the revenge.

What has caused humanity to say goodbye to the old world of spiritual experience or memory and to adopt the observation post of dead consciousness from which it saw the glory of the universe shrivel up and turn into a chilly machine, and the glory of the human being into a tortured piece of dust? Does this "fall into sin of the intellect" make any sense or should we, with Eduard von Hartmann, take the view that it would be better if the entire earth, with all that is on it, were to disappear?

It appears as if the evolution of humanity has to go through this stage. Materialism is not some accidental phenomenon in history, and in a hidden manner, perhaps completely unconsciously, Shakespeare makes its meaning clear to us.

With its pictures of death and darkness, his tragedy of the Danish prince is indeed a powerful warning to all of humanity to learn to recognize materialism as a stream that brings ruin and destruction. Nevertheless, this prince himself convinces us so strongly of the reality of the individual human being as a spiritual entity that, at the end of the tragedy, we know for certain that he is immortal. We know that his suffering and death are the trials which his "noble mind" had to go through in order to make progress on the path of development.

I have called it the Hamlet problem: the setting of an insurmountable boundary of consciousness between the knowable, physical-sensory world and the unknowable, spiritual world. The tragedy solves this problem only indirectly by giving the spectator the feeling that the immortal spirit does indeed exist, in spite of dark, physical death. Only in Shakespeare's later works will we find a direct answer to the Hamlet problem. In time we will discover this answer.

Hero, spectator, adept

Nowhere in the drama does Hamlet fall into such a state of self-contempt and rage as at the end of the second act. The "actor" has just given proof of his competence by reciting Priam's death and the consequent horror of Hecuba. This touches the actor himself so deeply that the color fades from his face, tears well up in his eyes and his voice breaks. Hamlet compares this acted emotion "about nothing—about Hecuba" with his own paralyzed ability to take action in a situation that should cause a far greater emotion in him than in a mere play-actor. It is yet another stroke of Shakespeare's poetic genius to place this outburst directly following a passage that evokes the destruction of Troy.

The process of the change in consciousness, spoken of in previous sections, evolved in stages. The Greeks, the trailblazers of modern times, developed a culture of the intellect which, it is true, did not yet carry the element of death as deeply as our civilization. But it did very clearly say goodbye to the older, pre-reflective societies. The war of Troy and the destruction of that city are therefore, in this context, to be viewed as the victory of a new, rational consciousness over an old, blood-related, theocratic consciousness. It is as if the pictures of the murdered Priam and the "mobled queen" Hecuba evoke in Hamlet a deeply buried memory in which a prince, still guided by the blood and not tormented by consciousness, valiantly fought, conquered or perished in accordance with the will of the gods—a prince who died a hero before his old father was atrociously murdered.

This certainty of will is what impresses Hamlet so much in young Fortinbras, "whose spirit with divine ambition puff'd ...," one of those men of the deed who "for a fantasy and trick of fame go to their graves like beds ..."—again, we see that Hamlet can speak only of "a fantasy" and not of a genuine impulse of will. He is no longer a hero because he no longer believes in the interrelationships of things, he no longer carries certainty in his blood but, instead, uncertainty in his brain.

As the Trojan hero Hector sealed the demise of an old era with his heroic death, so must Hamlet, by his unheroic demise, usher in a new era—our era—the power of which resides in the intellect that observes things from outside, but is powerless with respect to a deed dictated by the blood.

After having developed this spectator consciousness for over four centuries, we are hardly aware that the intellect makes cowards of us all, meaning that it makes us weak in our *moral will*. We are proud of the intellect because it has brought us great results in science and technology, but if we are honest we have to admit that these results fetter us more and more to materiality, and create ever greater distance from moral reality. The reality of the world is more than the physical aspect of things, and out of our spectator consciousness humanity will have to come to this insight in a new form. We cannot turn back our evolution; we must now, out of our own individual power of thinking, discover the certainty of the existence of a moral world order which in olden times we found dreamlike in our blood. The ancient blood morality is no longer valid. Spectator consciousness has brought with it the freedom of the individual human being. Our thoughts are free, but not toll-free! If we direct our thoughts exclusively toward material things, we will pay the toll of materialism: death and poisoning. However, if we courageously project our thoughts across the supposed boundary of the unknowable, then we discover the relation of our own spiritual reality with the spiritual-moral reality of the world. Only then can our deeds bring life, and not just death.

Hamlet is not yet capable of this. He still lives in the very beginning phase of the new consciousness that is tied to matter. It is his task, as a tragic human being, to show the world the consequences of this stage:

suffocation of the spirit, death and poison, poison and death.

He stands in the cemetery holding Yorick's skull in his hand. He loved this old jester of his father, but his love is not able to see beyond the perishable earthly remains and perceive the eternal spirit of this human being. He remains a spectator of the physical; his thoughts do not take flight across the limit of consciousness, but turn down with some emotion and chilly expressions of cynicism and mockery:

> Alas, poor Yorick! I knew him, Horatio; a fellow of infinite jest, most excellent fancy. He hath bore me on his back a thousand times; and now, how abhorred in my imagination it is! My gorge rises at it. Here hung those lips that I have kissed I know not how oft. Where be your gibes now? Your gambols? Your songs? Your flashes of merriment, that were wont to set the table on a roar? Not one now, to mock your own grinning? Quite chopfallen? Now get you to my lady's chamber, and tell her, let her paint an inch thick, to this favor she must come. Make her laugh at that. Prithee, Horatio, tell me one thing.
> *Horatio:* What's that, my lord?
> *Hamlet:* Dost thou think Alexander looked o' this fashion i' the earth?
> *Horatio:* E'en so.
> *Hamlet:* And smelt so? Pah! (*Throws down the skull.*)
> [5.1]

Goethe created a grand counterimage to this Hamlet scene with his poem *Lines on Seeing Schiller's Skull.* There he opens a way for modern human beings to reconnect with spiritual reality out of their spectator consciousness. Goethe's entire life and work testify to his striving to overcome the "Hamlet stage" of the death bringing consciousness. The poem gives ample proof of this:

Within a gloomy charnel-house one day
I view'd the countless skulls, so strangely mated,
And of old times I thought, that now were grey.
Close pack'd they stand, that once so fiercely hated,
And hardy bones, that to the death contended,
Are lying cross'd—to lie forever, fated.
What held those crooked shoulder blades suspended?
No one now asks; and limbs with vigour fired,
The hand, the foot—their use in life is ended.
Vainly ye sought the tomb for rest when tired;
Peace in the grave may not be yours; ye're driven
Back into daylight by a force inspired;
But none can love the wither'd husk, though even
A glorious noble kernel it contained.
To me, an adept, was the writing given
Which not to all its holy sense explained,
When 'mid the crowd, their icy shadows flinging,
I saw a form, that glorious still remained.
And even there, where mould and damp were clinging,
Gave me a blest, a rapture-fraught emotion,
As though from death a living fount were springing.
What mystic joy I felt! What rapt devotion!
That form, how pregnant with a godlike trace!
A look, how did it whirl me, tow'rd that ocean
Whose rolling billows mightier shapes embrace!
Mysterious vessel! Oracle how dear!
Even to grasp thee is my hand too base,
Except to steal thee from thy prison here
With pious purpose, and devoutly go
Back to the air, free thoughts, and sunlight clear.
What greater gain in life can man e'er know
Than when God-Nature will to him explain
How into Spirit steadfastness may flow,
How steadfast, too, the Spirit-Born remain.*

---

* J. W. von Goethe, *Bei Betrachtung von Schillers Schaedel* (*Lines on*

Why does a source of life rise up for Goethe out of death when he contemplates the physical remains of Schiller? It is because he does not view death on earth as an end. Schiller's spirit is alive: Goethe merely holds the instrument in his hand through which this spirit had worked on earth. He sees in all things physical the imprint of the spirit: "That form, how pregnant with a godlike trace!" All his life he practiced being a loving spectator of all earthly phenomena. For such a view the earth is not "a sterile promontory" and the air not filled with "pestilential vapors." Rather this earthly world becomes a revelation of the spirit.

The observer does not stand outside the phenomena, but these begin to speak a language he understands in his inner being: "Does not the core of the human being lie in the heart?"† His outer look awakens his inner gaze to the ocean of the spirit world in which archetypal images live in constant streaming. He is filled with deepest reverence because "God-Nature will to him explain." In this poem Goethe already describes what he later expresses as the keystone of his wisdom in the final chorus of his *Faust*:

> All things transitory
>
> But as symbols are they sent ...‡

He too stands in the cemetery as a spectator, just like Hamlet, but his gaze crosses the limits of consciousness. His contemplation of outer reality is at the same time a communion with the inner reality of things. The spectator has become an adept, an initiate who is capable of beneficent deeds. The way of Hamlet becomes the way of Faust. The end of Faust's life is filled with a beneficent

---

Seeing Schiller's Skull, www.poemhunter.com).

† J. W. von Goethe, *Gott und Welt: Ultimatum*, (tr. P.M)

‡ J. W. von Goethe, *Faust A Tragedy*, Part II, tr. Bayard Taylor, The Modern Library, New York, 1950.

work: the reclamation of the sea. But Goethe is aware of the fact that human beings who in our time go the way of Faust, from the consciousness of the spectator to that of the adept, have to accept the power of the dark companion Mephistopheles. Even in Faust's beneficent deeds Mephistopheles does not leave him alone, but Faust shows us the strength of the resurrection of the will that vanquishes this power in death:

> The noble spirit is now free,
> And saved from evil scheming
> Whoe'er aspires unweariedly
> Is not beyond redeeming.*

This is sung by the angels who receive Faust's entelechy in the spiritual spheres.

At Hamlet's death, Horatio speaks from an earthly viewpoint as a believing philosopher who can consider heaven merely as a place of rest after "the slings and arrows of outrageous fortune":

> Now cracks a noble heart. Good night, sweet prince,
> And flights of angels sing thee to thy rest! [5.2]

Shakespeare's inferno: disintegration of the soul

In his masterly book *Shakespeare's Prophetic Mind,* A.C. Harwood calls the tragedy of Hamlet a meditation on death. He calls attention to the many passages in which death is mentioned. Only, it is always death as the end, death as not-to-be, death without resurrection.

Between his thirty-fifth and forty-second years Shakespeare must have undergone strong death experiences. It is the period in which his great tragedies came into being: *Hamlet, Othello, Macbeth, King Lear.* It is not unlikely that the darkness which comes to us like a deluge out of these mighty tragedies had its cause in a fathomless grief that overshadowed his soul. We can only

---

* Ibid.

guess when we try to make a connection between this grief and the "dark lady" and the "fair youth" from his sonnets.

From these sublime poems, with their unmistakably autobiographical character, we know that Shakespeare in this period of his life had a deep friendship with a young nobleman and also suffered through a passionate love for a *femme fatale*. He surrendered with as much dedication to his "angel" as to his "demon" by which he was inwardly torn, particularly since he had to experience that this woman robbed him of both friend and love by deceiving him with this friend.

It is as if this life experience leads him to a sort of inferno, a world of hell. Shakespeare had arrived "midway life's journey," as Dante called it, i.e. his thirty-fifth year. Every human being then enters into a time of crisis because the curve of life begins to turn down. Human beings of that age have truly become citizens of the earth, their "I" forces have been fully unfolded, but as individuals they are now lonely, thrown back onto themselves in the world. Until that time they were carried by their physical and psychic forces; one could say, they went before the wind in their development. This now changes, and they must start making their way by the strength of their own self. Dante described this condition as being lost in a dark wood. He wants to climb the mountain of the spiritual realm, but is held back by three ominous beasts. He cannot ascend; he has to make a detour through the depths and descends into an inferno. The three beasts are the evil counter-images of his own soul forces. By his inferno experiences the catharsis is prepared that grows in him during his further journey through the spirit realm.

The midpoint of Shakespeare's life is also marked by the most intense trials of the soul, and we find the footprints of his inferno experiences in the four tragedies mentioned above, in the mighty dramatic images of an equally grim and awe-inspiring beauty as the inferno images of the Italian poet. What occurs in these four dramas is the disintegration of the human soul. In *Hamlet, Othello,* and *King Lear* we see how the three soul functions—thinking, feeling, and the will—are impaired by a "dislocation." In Hamlet, the student, thinking is debilitated because it can no longer penetrate to the spirit. In Othello, the warrior, feeling has turned into murderous rage by the infection of jealousy. In old King Lear rages the tempest of blind will, impulsive deeds without insight, without deliberation; he is the counter-pole to Hamlet. And always it is an innocent, loving female figure—Ophelia, Desdemona, Cordelia—who perishes by the "dislocation" in the principal male character.

The imagery speaks for itself. Is not the young woman the archetypal image of the soul in all fairy tales, sagas, and myths? In the sense of the Greek tragedies, Ophelia, Desdemona, and Cordelia are not tragic figures because they are not at the same time guilty and innocent. They have no guilt at all, and for this reason the deaths of these three "sisters" is so distressing, so horribly merciless. All three of them die because they cannot breathe: Ophelia by drowning, Desdemona by strangulation, and Cordelia by being hanged.

It is no coincidence that people have always perceived a close connection between soul and breath, and sometimes even used the same word for both. The soul, *anima*, lives in the flow of breath in us. At birth it comes in with the first inbreath, at death it leaves the body with the last outbreath. Soul emotions express themselves immediately in the movement of the breath; in tension, fright, and attention we hold our breath, when we relax we breathe out. Soul and breath form a unity, like form and content in a work of art. When the poet lets his principal female character die in a way that cuts off the breath he says in effect: the soul is being suffocated.

Suffocation of the soul being is the hallmark of Shakespeare's most moving tragedies. He must have experienced such suffocation as an inner trial in order to be able to portray it so dramatically. The archetypal image of the eternal feminine, so sunny, noble, triumphant, and dear, so tender and strong as it shines out to us in Juliet, Portia, Rosalind, Viola—all this now seems split in two. The woman is either a doomed angel or a devil. The strong devil lives in Lady Macbeth, the weak one in Hamlet's mother: "frailty thy name is woman."

Later Shakespeare will rediscover the eternal feminine in its untainted purity by the power of resurrection in his own soul. In *The Winter's Tale, Cymbeline*, even in the strange play of *Pericles, Prince of Tyre*, which is only partly of his hand, the soul purified in suffering meets us in the form of the woman risen from death. Moreover, in *The Winter's Tale, Pericles,* and *The Tempest* we meet three incomparably sweet and pure girls—Perdita, Marina, and Miranda—as the "rebirths" of Ophelia, Desdemona, and Cordelia. It would be interesting to examine the relationships of these three pairs of women, but that would go beyond the framework of our current study.

Nowhere does the demise of the soul receive such emphasis as in *Hamlet*, for here we see her being buried. The poet transports us to a cemetery, a "Place of the Skull" from where no resurrection takes place.

The gravediggers are, as *dramatis personae*, not indicated by the name of their work, but by the word "clown." When we watch a clown in a circus we usually do not realize that the origin of these tragic-comic jesters lies in the medieval allegorical morality plays. In these the *doomed human soul* was decked out with a peaked hat that symbolized a hell's crown, white or grey clothes, and a face painted white in which mouth and eyes appeared as big frightening holes.

In *Hamlet,* Shakespeare, who surely must have seen such allegorical plays in Stratford-on-Avon, reduced the "clown" to his original state. The allegory has disappeared, but the spiritual reality that is being indicated comes to the fore even more clearly: we are in the world of the inferno.

As the banquet scene in *Macbeth* is an evil counter-image of the Last Supper, the scene in the cemetery of Elsinore is a counter-image of Golgotha. On Golgotha, John stands under the cross. He is told to look after Mary in whom the archetypal image of the soul made its highest appearance on earth. Later, on Patmos, John sees this archetypal image of the Virgin as a cosmic imagination. His eagle spirit reaches to the highest worlds; his heart is most deeply filled with love. He can prophecy to humanity the Revelation of the world's end as the fulfillment of spiritual glory, as the resurrection of the dead.

Hamlet denied his love for his soul bride and thus gave her up to death. The human soul has suffocated, died, and was buried. The skulls of the dead come to light, but in the skulls of the living, the light of the spirit is extinguished. The priest refuses the sacrament; no redemption is possible.

Hamlet's thoughts do not take the flight of the eagle into the heights, but remain flat on the physical earth like dry scorpions. A battle of scorpions with a poisoned foil as mortal sting is the duel between Hamlet and Laertes. And this is the end of the drama!

Now we understand perhaps why modern human beings recognize themselves more easily in Hamlet than in Faust. The Hamlet being still dominates our culture; the Johannine Faust being who is allowed to discern the archetypal image of the Virgin in his "ascension" is something we still have to fulfill. But before Goethe, Shakespeare had already shown us in his last works a way to a salutary future. Nowhere did his "prophetic mind" indicate the mortal danger of the skull-bound consciousness more seriously and more grandly than in *Hamlet*; but this same spirit brings us in his "rising-from-death" tales the life-giving elixir of the resurrection.

5

As You Like It

Alchemy of the Soul

The other place

In the Greek tragedies and comedies we find the law of the three unities: the unity of place, time, and action. One concentrated dramatic story takes place within 24 hours in one and the same spot. In Shakespeare's works this is never the case. The course of the dramatic events involves continual changes of location, nor is the unity of time adhered to: sometimes days, months, or even years pass between acts.

Disregarding lesser changes in place such as "a different room in the palace," "elsewhere in the wood," etc., we may observe that with Shakespeare real changes in place often have to do with a polarity, i.e. two locations which have an existential but uneasy relationship with each other. We find a clear example of this in *The Merchant of Venice*, where Venice and Belmont are in every respect each other's counter-images. In *The Winter's Tale* the contrast between Sicily and Bohemia is striking.

A polarity distinguishes itself from a duality in that in the case of a polarity there is always a distinct middle realm. There is something curious about this middle realm. Actually, it is not something tangible; it is a tension between the two poles not unlike the interval between two tones. It arises as a *process*, as the two poles exert their influence on each other; it is mediation, reconciliation. In the drama, the principal characters go from one location to the other, and often back again. A process of development is enacted ending in reconciliation with a happy or tragic conclusion.

In Greek drama there is also a polarity, but it is not geographical. There we experience a tension between above and below, between the world of the gods and that of humanity. The polarity is a vertical one, while with Shakespeare it is horizontal: a contrast within earthly space.

And yet, we would make a mistake if we thought that this geographical contrast is to be viewed only as horizontal, simply as another country, another spot on the earth. One of the poles also encompasses the vertical element. It is a place "out of the world" such as Belmont, the Athenian wood, the flourishing land on the coast of Bohemia, and also the Forest of Arden in *As You Like It*. Swinburne calls it "the half heavenly Forest of Arden" in his wonderful *Introduction to the Works of Shakespeare*.

These areas are a kind of *mystery place*: the sun palace of Portia, the moon wood of Oberon and Titania, the island of Prospero. A mystery place is indeed somewhere on earth—one can travel there—but the place itself is hallowed, meaning that in this spot a connection with higher powers is possible; it is a concentration point of vertical connections between the human being and the spiritual world.

The archetype of this polarity, in which the one pole has the character of earthliness and death, and the other that of paradisal life and spiritual fullness, is to be found on *earth*, namely in the contrast between the biblical landscapes of Judea and Galilee. Judea is a wild, desolate desert with the city of Jerusalem and a few inhabitable oases, with the barren Jordan valley and the Dead Sea hundreds of feet below normal sea level. And Galilee has its rural settlements, its magical wealth of vegetation, its lake full of fish, its fertile fields.

The gospels relate that during his life Jesus continuously went back and forth between these two areas. His parents went from Nazareth in Galilee to Bethlehem in Judea where he was born. He spent his youth in Galilee. The baptism in the Jordan took place in Judea. Then he returned to Galilee where the first disciples joined him. And thus it went on, back and forth, until his last journey to Judea where he died, but where also the resurrection took place. After the resurrection we hear of Galilee again—John described the miraculous catch of fish in the Sea of Galilee—but it is likely that the disciples had remained in Jerusalem, and that what is indicated is an inner condition of raised consciousness.

As Greek tragedy arose out of the mystery of the suffering god-man Dionysus, whose true being was still kept hidden from the uninitiated by temple secrecy, so Christian drama originated in the liturgical passion and resurrection play in which the Christ mystery was shown to the faithful as the fulfillment of the ancient temple initiations. The events in Palestine at the beginning of our era are in their essence the archetypal drama that was not *played*, but actually *lived* for us.

The coming and going between Galilee and Judea is an integral part of this drama. The process of the God becoming man and the man becoming God is enacted in this repeated movement. Christ is the true mediator between the polarity of Judea and Galilee, death and life, earth and heaven. The geographical contrast between these two landscapes is not only concretely observable; it is at the same time a reflection of a much greater, spiritual polarity, namely the contrast between the world of the fall into sin, the earth, and Paradise.

It should be no surprise that in the greatest dramatic poet since the Greek tragedians we encounter the Christian motif of *traveling over the earth*, coming and going between two areas, between a place of oppression and affliction and a place of catharsis and fulfillment, between "sinful" earth and innocent paradise which has to be renewed and realized on earth. Indeed, is not the whole of Christian literature filled with this motif? Consciously or unconsciously, all of humanity is moving forward in the process of the *Imitatio Christi*.

However, the "other place," the place "out of the world," is never presented as a realm of absolute bliss; at best it can develop into this if certain trials have been endured. Human beings who seek fulfillment are here tried on the strength of their *love*. Bassanio, Orlando, Florizel, and Ferdinand pass their trials and are then worthy of uniting in marriage with the beloved Virgin.

Also "this side," the place of sin and sorrow, Venice, Sicily, the Duke's court, is not only a place of evil. Here light and darkness are also mixed. At the court of the tyrant, radiant Rosalind and sweet Celia are living like white doves in a colony of crows. In Shylock's house lives winsome Jessica; in Sicily, ravaged by tyranny and mourning, shines the unwavering soul force of Paulina.

There is one dramatic figure—he is completely missing in ancient Greek drama, but we do find him in Indian drama—that frolics through both polar realms without undergoing any change at all: the *jester*, the *absurd*. The "clown" or "fool" is invulnerable, inviolable, unapproachable, incorrigible, incomparable. He is devoted without real love; he is wise without true morality; he connects everything and everyone without entering into a real relationship with anyone. Even when he gets married, he really does not want to be "well married," so that he will later have a good excuse to get rid of his wife.

The jester is the most mysterious figure in the drama, just as humor is the most mysterious force on earth. Humor is surely something divine, and yet I cannot picture heaven as humorous. Humor has surely also something to do with the devil, and yet I know that true humor chases the devil away. The funniest thing about humor is that it cannot be learned. I have never met a person who had *developed* humor. Either we are born with the jester in us, or we aren't.

Humor is Amor with a mask; he shoots arrows that make us laugh. We see reality shifted off-center just a bit, and that makes it possible to bear the unbearableness of reality. That is why in the realm of oppression, as well as in the realm of fulfillment, the jester is always himself. Still, the jester also has something melancholy. When he momentarily lifts the mask of humor a little, we can see the tear-stained face of Amor. Why does Amor weep? Because the original wholeness of the world has been broken into realities. Just listen to the most beautiful, most melancholy fool's song that was ever written. Feste, the clown in *Twelfth Night* sings at the end of the play:

When that I was a little tiny boy,
With hey, ho, the wind and the rain,
A foolish thing was but a toy,
For the rain it raineth every day.

But when I came to man's estate,
With hey, ho, the wind and the rain,
'Gainst knave and thief men shut their gate,
For the rain it raineth every day.

But when I came, alas, to wive,
With hey, ho, the wind and the rain,
By swaggering could I never thrive,
For the rain it raineth every day.

But when I came unto my bed,
With hey, ho, the wind and the rain,

With toss-pots still had drunken head,
For the rain it raineth every day.
A great while ago the world began,
With hey, ho, the wind and the rain,
But that's all one, our play is done,
And we'll strive to please you every day. [5.1]

In the study of *Hamlet* it was pointed out that the clown is originally the damned human soul. In this connection it is significant that in Shakespeare the comedy fools usually accompany one of the principal female parts, unlike the buffoon-like Sancho in *Don Quixote*, Papageno in *The Magic Flute*, or Sganarelle in *Don Juan*, who accompany the principal male parts. Shakespeare places the "tear-stained" soul with the mask of humor side by side with, or opposite, the "heavenly" soul which, undergoing earthly trials, has to find its connection with the "bridegroom," the spirit.

Perhaps we will solve the question of the jester if we can probe the theme of this study of *As You Like It: alchemy of the soul*, in sufficient depth. For the riddle of humor, it seems to me, is an alchemical riddle. In this connection, we have to say a few words about the "Forest of Arden" before we proceed to the description of the content of this comedy.

It is clear that this "merry wood" is one of those places that form a contrast with areas of sorrow. Here Shakespeare sets the evil world of humanity and the court with its perfidiousness, violence, and tyranny over against the world of nature, where there may be storm or frost, but it still makes a "jolly life" possible. Except for the first act and a few brief scenes in Acts II and III, the play is set in this environment of nature. It is called a pastoral comedy, just as Shakespeare's source, *Rosalynde* by Lodge, is called a pastoral tale in prose.

The pastoral, the scene of shepherds that is set in an idyllic, Arcadian landscape, was greatly *en vogue* in Shakespeare's day. The genre remained popular well into the eighteenth century, and no matter how inane and contrived it often was, it had the widest possible appeal to readers and spectators. This magic of the Arcadian pictures is understandable because the origin of the pastoral is not inane at all. The symbol of the shepherd is as old as humanity. Shepherds are simple, uncultured people with a *loving heart*. They live in virgin nature and tend sheep and lambs, the images of the untainted soul. In sacred language, therefore, the shepherd becomes the guardian of the soul, the priest.

The enemy of the shepherd is the wolf, the image of evil, especially dangerous when it disguises itself in sheep's clothing. In paradise, the evil one is the tempter clothed as innocence. In Indian mythology we find the shepherd god Krishna in the paradisal sphere of love and fertility. In these pictures we are struck by a strongly erotic element; however, with the ancient Indians this was still pure and not egoistic. The realm of the loving shepherds is truly paradise, the realm of the Tree of Life.

Shakespeare touched everything he adopted from his contemporaries and predecessors with a magic wand. Not only are his pastorals in the Forest of Arden or along the coast of Bohemia deliciously light and sunny, he also knows how to conjure the archetypal image of this realm before our eyes. He creates a new mythology! In the chapter on *The Winter's Tale* we will have occasion to come back to the theme of the pastoral.

Shakespeare was a child of nature. From rural Stratford he went to the big city, London, and threw himself into the bustle of the culture; he lived and worked there where the pulse of a new era was beating. But he never forgot the unspoilt hills and woods of the area where he was born. The extent of his bond with nature shows already from the fact that in his work around one hundred fifty names of plants and a hundred bird names are mentioned.

The nature of the Forest of Arden is characterized by something more than the traits of an Arcadian place of purity and love. It is a real English wood, with game and hunters, with singing birds and singing noblemen; with common birds and strange human birds: Touchstone, the spotted woodpecker; and Jaques, the splenetic crow; with noble virgins and an exiled prince; with a young lover and a deliciously dumb farm girl. And all these characters meet each other, avoid each other, find each other in sympathy or repel each other in antipathy.

The wood is a retort, a test-tube in which the chemicals are not substances but souls. It is the alchemical laboratory where the poet prepares the "Great Work" of the "Chymical Wedding" of souls, where the seven stages of the chymical process of soul development are enacted. In order to find this imaginative aspect of the comedy we must first sketch the outer course of events again.

The story

Act I

Orlando, a young nobleman, pours out his troubles to an old servant, Adam. His father, upon his death, left him a mere thousand crowns and entrusted him to the care of his brother Oliver. The latter has failed to give him his inheritance and treats him very badly.

Oliver appears and his rough words addressed to Orlando confirm the allegation. The brothers get into a fight. Oliver, who has keenly felt Orlando's grip on his throat, decides to cure him of his rebelliousness. A good opportunity presents itself for this when Charles, the duke's wrestler, reports that Orlando wants to pit his strength against him in a match. Oliver encourages the wrestler not to spare the young man.

In an open area in front of the palace, Celia, the daughter of Duke Frederick, and her niece Rosalind are in conversation with each other. Rosalind cannot forget her father who was dethroned and exiled by his brother Frederick. Celia consoles her and promises to return the stolen inheritance to Rosalind when her father dies. The conversation takes on a lighter tone and Touchstone, the jester, joins in with his witticisms.

Le Beau enters and tells the girls about the wrestling triumphs of Charles who has broken the rib cages of three husky young men. The last part of the match is going to take place just where the girls are talking. Orlando will wrestle with Charles. In vain, Rosalind and Celia try to talk him out of his intention. The match is won by Orlando. When he makes himself known to the Duke, the latter is upset, because Orlando's father had been against him. Frederick's unkind reaction is made good by the girls. Rosalind gives the speechless young nobleman a locket she was wearing. The way she looked at him floored the victor over Charles: he has fallen in love.

Le Beau comes in to warn him of the anger of the Duke and advises him to flee. When Orlando asks him which of the two girls is the daughter of the Duke, he tells him of the intimate friendship of the two nieces and of the danger that threatens Rosalind also. The Duke does not like her.

Indeed he doesn't. A raging Frederick barges into the room where the girls are talking about Orlando with whom Rosalind has, in her turn, fallen in love. Rosalind is summarily sent into exile, Celia's entreaties notwithstanding. Frederick is afraid of the love of the people and the court for the daughter of his dethroned brother, and that this loyalty might lead to mutiny against himself.

The girls now decide to go together to the Forest of Arden where Rosalind's father is living with a number of noblemen. Rosalind will disguise herself as a hunter named Ganymede and Celia will go with "him" as his sister named Aliena. They take Touchstone, the jester, with them.

Act II

In the Forest of Arden we meet the exiled duke. He praises the rugged but honest life on the land and his companions agree with him. We hear of Jaques, a melancholic gentleman who has compassion for a wounded deer.

Back at the court, we see Frederick extremely annoyed with the disappearance of his daughter. He suspects that Orlando is accompanying the two girls because an eavesdropping chambermaid heard them praise the young man. Frederick gives an order to bring Orlando to him from the house of his brother. Should he be gone, then Oliver must be brought before the Duke. Adam warns Orlando that his brother wants to kill him. They decide to flee together. Adam gives his young master the money he has saved.

Rosalind, Celia, and Touchstone have arrived in the wood, totally exhausted. They hear a conversation between an old and a young shepherd, Corin and Silvius. The latter is desperately in love with Phebe, who spurns his love. Rosalind asks the old shepherd for shelter. He will take them to a shepherd's cottage that is for sale together with meadows, a flock of sheep, a sheepfold, and himself as their servant. Rosalind makes the purchase.

Amiens, a nobleman in the retinue of the Duke, sings a song. Jaques, who evades the Duke because he argues too much with him, asks for the singing to continue. They all sing together, and Jaques recites a parody on the song.

Adam and Orlando have also arrived in the wood. The old servant is completely exhausted. Orlando leaves him behind while he goes to try and find something to eat for him. The Duke is having a meal in the wood with his companions. Jaques comes in all enthused because he has met a jester. Orlando abruptly intrudes into the group and demands food. The dignified reaction of the Duke puts him to shame. He explains his distress, is invited to the meal, then leaves to fetch old Adam.

Jaques proclaims his wisdom of human life in seven parts. Orlando returns with Adam. There is eating and singing. Orlando makes himself known, and the Duke is happy to have the son of his old friend with him.

Act III

Frederick orders Oliver to bring him his missing brother dead or alive. He confiscates all his possessions and chases him out of the court.

Orlando hangs love poems addressed to Rosalind on trees in the forest. Corin and Touchstone are having a strange conversation when Rosalind enters. She reads one of Orlando's verses to them. Touchstone mocks the verse. Celia has also found a poem stuck on a tree. She reads it and teases her niece with Orlando. Rosalind becomes excited when Celia tells her that she has seen him. Orlando enters with Jaques who is unimpressed by his doggerels. Rosalind addresses Orlando, but he does not recognize her. She offers to cure him of the pangs of his love. He has to call her—i.e. the youth Ganymede—Rosalind and come to the sheepfold every day to court his beloved.

Touchstone has hooked a pretty farm girl, Audrey, and wants to marry her. Jaques spies on the pair. A village priest appears to solemnize the marriage. Jaques offers to give away the bride but advises Touchstone to get married decently in church. The priest remains behind, confused when the threesome disappears.

Rosalind and Celia talk about Orlando who seems to lack the skills of a lover. They witness Silvius's pangs of love and Phebe's catty rejections. Rosalind-Ganymede defends the unhappy shepherd. She calls Phebe all kinds of names with the result that the latter falls in love with him/her. When Rosalind is gone, Phebe is filled with more gentle feelings, also for faithful Silvius.

Act IV

Jaques and Rosalind are in conversation. She reproaches him for his melancholy. When Orlando enters, Jaques leaves. The make-believe courtship leads to a charming, child-like wedding ceremony in which Celia functions as priest. Orlando has to leave for the meal with the Duke. Rosalind remains behind, sighing for his return. Silvius brings an "angry" letter from Phebe to Ganymede; it is an ardent declaration of love.

Oliver appears bringing a bloody handkerchief of Orlando who had saved his sleeping brother from certain death. Fighting with a lioness that was poised to jump on Oliver he was wounded. Oliver tells of his vicissitudes and how he came to see the error of his ways and recognized the evil in himself. At the story of Orlando's wound Rosalind faints. Oliver accompanies the girls to their house.

Act V

Touchstone has a rival: William. He gets rid of him in the manner of a jester. Oliver has fallen in love with Celia and wants to marry her as soon as possible. Orlando frets that he is not able to have such happiness. Rosalind promises him to bring him his bride tomorrow with the magic she claims to possess. Silvius and Phebe enter and Phebe upbraids Ganymede for showing her letter to Silvius. Silvius has to express what love is. The foursome now speaks a kind of love quartet. Rosalind promises to make them all happy tomorrow.

The next day the entire forest company is together. The Duke promises to give his daughter Rosalind to Orlando as his wife, if Ganymede can make her appear. Phebe promises that, if she no longer wants to marry Ganymede, she will become Silvius's wife. Silvius promises to take Phebe as his wife if she agrees. Jaques foresees a new Great Flood because all animals come to the ark in pairs. Two very strange beasts are now approaching: Touchstone with his Audrey. Touchstone explains the seven degrees of the noble contest concerning the nature of lying.

Hymen, the god of marriage, appears together with Rosalind dressed in a woman's gown and Celia. Orlando recognizes his beloved; Phebe realizes her mistake and consoles herself with Silvius. The Duke joyfully greets his daughter and niece. Hymen unites the two happy pairs.

The youngest brother of Orlando and Oliver comes in with the report that Duke Frederick, who was on his way to the forest with an army to catch his brother and kill him, has been converted by a wise hermit he met at the edge of the wood. He renounces the world, gives crown and dukedom back to his brother, and returns all the possessions he had taken from people.

This news makes the Duke happy. He invites everyone to celebrate it with song and dance. Jaques is the only one who is not happy. He wants to visit the newly-baked convert Frederick and leaves with the good wishes of the Duke and the happy couples. The scene closes with a dance; Rosalind speaks the epilogue.

Process and spectator

When we thus place the dry content of this poetic masterwork before our eyes, we are struck by the fact that only in the first act, at the court of the Duke, does anything really dramatic take place. The other acts seem to be filled with talking, singing and more talking. And when something dramatic does happen, such as the rescue of Oliver from the threat of the snake and the lion, or the conversion of Duke Frederick, the event is merely related, just like the report of a messenger in a classical Greek tragedy. If we would call this a weakness of the play we would completely disregard the essence of this comedy.

When we enter the Forest of Arden we truly step into a different world. It is significant that Shakespeare, who in general closely follows the story by Lodge, makes a change in regard to the outcome for Frederick. In Lodge's story the tyrant is killed in a battle. Shakespeare gives him a better life by his encounter with an old, pious man when he has come "to the skirts of the wild wood." Oliver also comes to himself in the wood, and is cured of his malevolence.

The wood is not a place of outer events such as family quarrels, wrestling matches or chasing away innocent girls; it is a place of inner movement. And this inner movement comes to expression in the many encounters and conversations, or in the reports related in pictures of an inner change.

Oliver does describe his adventure as an external event: as he lay sleeping, a snake had wound itself around his neck and a lioness was poised to jump on him when he woke up. But a snake and a lioness in a place where "the icy fang and churlish chiding of the winter's wind—bites and blows," may well be viewed as pictures of Oliver's inner ill nature. At the level of imagination, the snake of jealousy and the lion of violence are no strangers to us.

It is interesting that the snake immediately vanishes when Orlando appears, without doing any damage; with the lion, however, he has to fight. He is himself not yet free of the vice of violence, witness his wild entrée at the meal of the Duke. He vanquishes the lion, but incurs a wound. It is without any doubt the intention of the poet to present the wood as a place of inner trial, catharsis, separation, and attachment.

There is not a single outer reason why Rosalind would not right away go to her father in the wood, or immediately make herself known to her beloved Orlando. A philistine will view the make-believe courtship between Orlando and Rosalind, the sudden love of Phebe for a boy who is no boy, the spontaneous changes in Oliver and Frederick as nothing but improbable, complicated, and superfluous nonsense. But that is because such a person does not understand that all the figures in the play inwardly belong together—they are in essence one figure: the human being. Such a person cannot understand that Orlando can only marry Rosalind after his brother Oliver and Celia have found each other, and Phebe has accepted her faithful shepherd as her husband.

The final fulfillment does not come until the good has proved to be firm and sure, evil has been chastened, that which made false attachment has been loosened, and what really belongs together has joined together. In brief, a *process* has to take place.

There are two figures in the wood who, although they interact with others all the time, in fact remain outside the whole. They do not go through a catharsis in a true sense, nor do they forge a real attachment. Touchstone does marry Audrey, but we know already: this attachment won't last long. Jaques congratulates everyone, but he walks out of the celebration to visit the converted tyrant. He does not do this out of unkindness, but out of curiosity; he thinks he will be able to learn something from such a person.

Touchstone, the merry spectator and commentator, and Jaques, the melancholy spectator and commentator, are actually real egoists, and, as such, they can well appreciate each other. The spectator of the process stands outside the process. The melancholic Jaques is a herald of *Hamlet*. Touchstone and Jaques do not figure in Lodge's story; together with Audrey and William, the duffer, they are original inventions of Shakespeare.

In the first section I compared the Forest of Arden with an alchemical laboratory in which the poet prepares the "great work." Shakespeare, however, as creative soul alchemist, must have felt the need to introduce an element into the process which in reality is not part of it. It is the element of the critical spectator.

In our study of *Hamlet* we have given much attention to spectator consciousness. We have seen how this tragically leads to estrangement from the world and humanity. Jaques's comical sallies do not disguise this. In fact, he denies the development of the human being. He gives a sharply drawn picture of the seven stages of human life, but his conclusion is that the last phase, old age, is again like the first, that of the little child. The human being moves in a kind of circle without making progress. Jaques calls these stages "parts":

> All the world's a stage,
> And all the men and women merely players;
> They have their exits and their entrances;
> And one man in his time plays many parts,
> His acts being seven ages. At first the infant,
> Mewling and puking in the nurse's arms;
> Then the whining schoolboy, with his satchel

And shining morning face, creeping like snail
Unwillingly to school. And then the lover,
Sighing like furnace, with a woeful ballad
Made to his mistress's eyebrow. Then a soldier,
Full of strange oaths, and bearded like the pard,
Jealous in honour, sudden and quick in quarrel,
Seeking the bubble reputation
E'en in the cannon's mouth. And then the justice,
In fair round belly with good capon lin'd,
With eyes severe and beard of formal cut,
Full of wise saws and modern instances;
And so he plays his part. The sixth age shifts
Into the lean and slipper'd pantaloon,
With spectacles on nose and pouch on side;
His youthful hose, well sav'd, a world too wide
For his shrunk shank; and his big manly voice,
Turning again toward childish treble, pipes
And whistles in his sound. Last scene of all,
That ends this strange eventful history,
Is second childishness and mere oblivion;
Sans teeth, sans eyes, sans taste, sans everything. [2.7]

The most sublime specimen of sour wittiness ever concocted by a critical observer of life! By the way, it is interesting that Jaques still places the seven phases of life in clear connection with the planets, only he leaves the sun out! For him there are only six, because the seventh is a repetition of the first. Early youth: Moon; school age: Mercury; adolescence: Venus; early adulthood: Mars; mature adulthood: Jupiter; old age: Saturn. It would take us much too far to go deeper into the relationships between the phases of life and the planets; this is old mystery wisdom that was rejuvenated by modern anthroposophical spiritual science. Suffice it to observe that the Sun phase lies between the Venus and Mars phases (21–42 years of age) and that melancholy was of old the anti-Sun vice, which clearly plays a role in Jaques's dour view of life.

And Touchstone? Touchstone in essence denies marriage. His union with Audrey is really a joke, and therefore actually mean. He does the opposite of what Rosalind does. Rosalind gives Phebe, who loves her, to the one who really belongs to her, Silvius. Touchstone, however, for his own benefit takes Audrey away from her rightful lover William, the duffer. The nice parallel is that Rosalind cannot be a real husband for Phebe, and that William is but a "rotten lover" for Audrey. Shakespeare thus relativises the altruism of Rosalind and the egoism of Touchstone.

Shakespeare would not be Shakespeare without giving the negative element of the critical spectator also some humanity and warmth. Jaques, the pessimist who takes human life off its pedestal and hides the sun, is also deeply moved by compassion for the dying deer which, by the way, gives him a fresh occasion to scoff at people.

And Touchstone may not be overly particular with the morals of married life, but he is dear to us because of his faithfulness toward his mistress Celia and by his inimitable humor. We are hardly surprised that Jaques does not like Orlando, and Rosalind does not like Jaques. In the process that leads to their union, Jaques is, in a certain sense, a hurdle. But this hurdle is a human, and in a larger context also a historical reality.

Shakespeare heralds an era in which the old alchemy will be replaced by the science of critical observation. That this science will take the human being off his pedestal and turn its back on the glory of true humanity is something the unforgettable figure of "melancholy Jaques" can teach us.

Alchemy

It may seem like going too far to lay a connection between such a playful and radiant comedy and something which, at least in its origin, was extremely serious, but frequently something light and airy turns out to have a hidden serious significance.

If we want to understand alchemy we must first let go of some traditional notions, whether we view them as positive or negative. We must first forget about all gold-making, the philosopher's stone, the elixir of life, and other "miraculous" things. We should then go in our minds to the workroom of an alchemist from the *early* Middle Ages. There we see a human being with a tragically earnest face engaged with complete dedication in what we would call a chemical experiment. In his test tubes and retorts we recognize all kinds of substances: acids, metals, salts, organic and inorganic substances. We see solutions, crystallizations, evaporations, oxidations, and more of such things.

However, should we be able to gaze into his soul, then we would discover something that would surprise us. In the first place, we would see a boundless religious devotion; in the second place, a tragic mood. If we should show him in our life and thinking habits that we would be worthy of becoming his pupils, he would speak to us in words like the following:

> "In my test-tubes and retorts, in my fiery oven, I connect substances from nature with each other. I do this only after having prepared myself thoroughly in prayer and meditation. In a mood of complete surrender to higher powers I observe the processes that take place in my retorts with the question of how these processes occur in my own body and how they have their corresponding effect in nature at large.

"The beings that live in these processes then begin to speak to me. They reveal themselves in colors that change into humming sounds, into melodies and harmonies. And the nature spirits of the solid state and the fluid, gaseous, and fiery states, freed out of the mysterious working of the substances, speak to me, teach me.

"They show me how, given the intimate relationship between the processes that take place in us and outside us, I can prepare the remedies that can cure a disturbance in the human organism. With such medicaments I can serve people. But the ignorant ones, who think that I am wise and happy and powerful because of my art, do not realize the unbearable pains I suffer.

"True, the nature spirits, the gnomes, undines, sylphs, and salamanders; the spirits, respectively, of earth, water, air, and fire; share their secrets with me, but they are mere shadows of the high, sacred spirits of the stars, and their wisdom is only a picture of divine revelations which, in their direct form, have been lost to humanity. What the spirits of the stars once spoke to human beings in the sacred mystery centers in east, west, north, and south has fallen silent for our souls. I can only hear the humming and whispering of Nature, which preserves memories from primeval times. The Book of Heaven is closed to me.

"A time will come when the Book of Nature will also be closed to humanity. Then they will have only memories of memories in their self-made books, of which they will boast in ignorant pride."

If this alchemist was a real initiate he could have communicated many secrets to his pupil, secrets that were living experiences in olden times. He could then speak of gold in relation to the sun in the cosmos and to thinking in the microcosm of the human being. And he would speak of the philosopher's stone—carbon—which, unlike gold, combines with oxygen. He still knew that at one time the cosmic spirits of the moon revealed to human beings, who had been prepared for this, that carbon in its diverse forms outside us—diamond, anthracite, graphite—and within us—carbon dioxide—only appears in those forms on earth. On the moon, this same substance is silver. And he would teach his pupil a profound contemplation of substance as the virginal *primeval mother of all things*, who reveals herself in endless varieties of forms but is forever the holy carrier of the eternal creative Word.

What I have described here is a concise rendering of statements by Rudolf Steiner about the old medieval alchemy.* He calls attention to the relationship the true alchemists still had with the nature spirits, and that the wisdom in which they were thus able to share was a mere *picture* of the divine world, no longer a direct revelation such as was possible in ancient mystery centers like Samothrace, Eleusis, or Hibernia. He calls the laboratories of the early Middle Ages as described above mystery centers of the Rosicrucians, and indicates with this that the movement that later became known under this name in Europe had a much earlier origin than is generally thought. Finally, he emphasizes that what was later called alchemy was a decadent form compared with the original impulse, which explains why this later alchemy could easily degenerate into illusion and charlatanism.

---

* See R. Steiner, *Mystery Knowledge and Mystery Centres*, CW 232, Rudolf Steiner Press, 2013.

Alchemy was renowned from the fourteenth and fifteenth centuries to the beginning of the nineteenth century. It was not the gold makers and charlatans, but the real adepts in this art who belonged to the occult brotherhood of the Rose Cross, or they were inspired by the spiritual leader of this brotherhood (see the next section). Their striving was for a *renewal of the ancient mystery wisdom in a Christianized form*.

For the period indicated above, alchemy was the appropriate form for this. It is no longer so in our time. In anthroposophical spiritual science we find a metamorphosis of this striving in a form that responds to the situation of humanity today. As to the still-existing Rosicrucian societies, we leave them out of consideration; this is not the place to go into them.

In his lectures given in Neuchatel, Switzerland in 1911, Rudolf Steiner spoke of alchemy as follows.† The Rosicrucian distinguished three great processes in nature. In the first place, there is *salt formation*. Everything that precipitates from a solution as solid substance, which forms itself, he called *salt*. However, he did not look at such a process from outside; rather, the observation of the salt process became an inner experience for him that worked like a prayer in his soul. He knew that lower instincts, passions, and desires were continually working in him like a process of decomposition, inner putrefaction. If human beings wish to protect themselves from this and overcome their lower nature, which is the cause of all illness, they must devote themselves to noble thoughts that are directed to the spirit.

What is salt formation in nature is, in the soul, the

---

† See R. Steiner, *The Reappearance of Christ in the Etheric,* Steiner-Books, new edition forthcoming.

victory of spirituality over the forces that lead to decay. Rosicrucians revered in deepest piety and surrender the divine powers that revealed themselves through the veil of the natural process. He felt himself at one with the pure divine thoughts of the macrocosm when he evoked in himself the purity of spiritual thinking, which the intense experience of the salt process stimulated in him.

The second important process the alchemist pursued in his experiments was *dissolution*. Everything that can bring something else to dissolution was called *mercury*. Which force in the human soul corresponds with the dissolution process? It is the power of love. As there exist lower and higher dissolution processes, so we can also distinguish lower and higher forms of love. The witnessing of the dissolution process again became a pious prayer: as divine love has worked in the world for aeons of time, so love works in the human soul.

The third process was *combustion*. Everything that can go up in flames was called *sulphur* by the alchemist. The corresponding cosmic power is that of ardent surrender to the Godhead. The Rosicrucian alchemist saw in the stages of development of the earth a process of slowly progressing purification, a combustion process. At some time the earth will be purified by heavenly, apocalyptic fire. Divine beings work here who dedicate themselves to still higher beings.

All combustion may only be carried out in the alchemical laboratory when the deepest religious feelings, the highest readiness to sacrifice, are living in the soul of the alchemist. For in combustion he saw the sacrifice of the gods to the highest God.

In this way the experiments with physical processes brought about a gradual development of the highest soul forces, and an awareness grew of the relationship between these and the highest forces in the world-all. In salt formation: *divine thoughts*; in dissolution: *divine love*; in combustion: *divine sacrifice.*

Those who advanced on this path full of trials and dramatic inner experiences experienced a catharsis of the soul that came to expression in the color of the auras of such individuals. In this psychic radiation, which can only be clairvoyantly perceived, the shades of color changed as the process of perfection progressed. In the unfolding of divine-pure thoughts in the salt process, the aura became *copper* colored; in the divine-love force of the dissolution process, *silver* shone in the aura; and finally, in combustion, the divine sacrifice, *gold* would radiate out.

Thus the true alchemists "made gold," subjective gold, by filling themselves completely with purity, love, and the power of sacrifice. This growing inner fullness opened their higher organs of perception so that they became able to see through the veil of nature and perceive the workings of spiritual beings and how these bring about the growth and decay of the things of the world. In this way they also obtained insight into the forces of the human soul—which forces lead to disintegration and decay, and which to growth and rejuvenation. They learned to know the law of death and resurrection as an inner experience.

The wisdom which the Rosicrucians thus acquired was expressed in certain signs and figures. These were not so much symbols but rather imaginative pictures as these can be observed in a higher state of consciousness. Such signs and figures were not made known until a hundred years had passed.

Modern psychology, especially that of Jung, is on a completely wrong track when it wants to see images of sexuality in those alchemical imaginations that in one way or another have to do with the masculine and feminine. Subconscious passions and instincts is one area with which alchemy has absolutely nothing to do.

We may wonder whether the striving of the Rosicrucian alchemist was not primarily intended toward self-perfection for which the laboratory experiments were merely used to evoke a mystical experience. However, that is not the case. Alchemy is no mysticism. It distinguishes itself very clearly from the mystical path of schooling in which the divine was found in the depths of the soul, not in the working of nature.

As to self-perfection, this was entirely put in service of humanity. Not only did the Rosicrucian physician never charge for his medical help, his "hidden" work also had the character of service. The spiritual radiance that emanated from these highly developed individuals was unimaginably strong, although historical documents do not speak about this.

These people remained inconspicuous, they never took center stage, they received no fame or fortune. But they inspired and encouraged others. In the Middle Ages many folk tales originated from the source of alchemical wisdom. A number of interesting inventions, for instance, in the production of pottery and porcelain, came out of alchemy. Even in politics and social life they exerted a beneficent influence (see the next section).

The experiments themselves did not lead to inner experiences; they embodied the deepest meaning of the alchemical striving.

We have to realize that there is a difference in principle between a chemical and a chymical view of a substance—I am using the word "chymical" now for "alchemical." Modern chemistry knows matter only in its state of death. Through their intellect human beings are able to make this dead matter extremely useful today. For instance, they can make an artificial substance that *does not dissolve* and *does not burn*: plastic. The alchemist sought the spiritually indestructible; the modern chemist found the physically indestructible (with all the problems it causes).

The alchemist viewed matter, as we usually know it, as a product of the fall into sin, as the consequence of radical changes that have taken place in the development of the earth and humanity. If we want to penetrate to the essence of matter as it physically appears, we must look for the cause of its state of appearance in the human being. The original, "virginal," purity of matter, which used to be called *materia prima*, was still filled with *cosmic life*. In the beginning of our planetary evolution the human being still shared in this divine cosmic life. It was the element in which he "breathed." He was still living under the Tree of Life in the garden of Paradise.

In this condition the feminine and masculine principles were still united in one being. The human being was still androgynous, a hermaphrodite, in whose dreamlike, completely unfree consciousness the godliness of the world was mirrored. The fall into sin did not only cause a change in the human being (see the chapter on *Macbeth*), but it also changed matter. Cosmic life withdrew from human beings to the extent that they began to develop a free consciousness. Matter condensed and became less permeable for the spiritual. In this condensed materiality human beings could no longer live in their androgynous condition; the separation into man and woman took place.

Should earthly matter have been completely left to itself, without any influence of the divine, all life on earth would have disappeared long ago; the ever-progressing condensation process would have turned the earth into a slag heap.

Modern natural science admits the fact that the earth will in the end turn into a slag heap, but it does not recognize two important truths which the alchemists still knew, and which are renewed in anthroposophical spiritual science. Not only do human beings preserve something of the beginning cosmic condition in themselves—they still carry a hidden element of Paradise in their physical organism—but by their birth they continually bring spiritual substance into the material world. And at their death a spiritual element combines with the dying substance of the earth. In the decomposition of dead human bodies spirit enters into matter, with the result that life is able to continue. Here again we face the secret of growth and decay.

But this human-earthly process would still in the end lead to death, were it not that an infinitely higher power permeated the earthly world like a heavenly leaven. The gospel points to this higher power when it speaks of the event on Golgotha. The sacrificial blood of the Redeemer not only absolves humanity of its guilt due to the fall into sin, but it penetrates the substance of the earth as a spiritual power of resurrection, due to which the earth is able to develop in the future into a renewed, cosmically reborn earth, the New Jerusalem. Christ enables the human beings who connect themselves with him to overcome the consequences of the fall into sin. The process of catharsis of fallen humanity is concurrently the redemption of fallen matter.

In the experiment that in alchemical literature was called the Great Work the goal was the preparation of the so-called philosopher's stone, also indicated with the word "tincture" or "hermaphrodite." This chymical process took place in seven stages: *mortificatio*—dying; *putrefactio*—decomposition; *solutio*—dissolution;

animatio—ensoulment; *purefactio*—purification; *perfectio*—perfection; and *fixatio*—attachment. The last phase was often marked by the image of a wedding, the chymical wedding of a king and a queen, or of the mercury principle (dissolution) and sulphur, the combustion principle.

It was to the end product of this process, namely what came into being due to the chymical wedding, that all those miraculous characteristics were attributed (metal transformations, revivification, complete healing, etc.) which have been the subject of so much misunderstanding, deception, experiments and, finally, a neverending stream of books.

From the foregoing it will have become clear that the true Rosicrucian adepts were no wonder workers. The philosopher's stone was the secret of life in death and death in life. By certain procedures which one followed "synthetically" with natural substances, it was possible to grasp the creative spirit in world phenomena. This was only given to those who by their initiation had overcome the death force in their cognitional capacity, individuals who in their thinking, feeling, and deeds brought to realization divine crystal-clear purity, streaming love, and a burning power of sacrifice.

The "end product" of the chymical process, which in its sevenfold development corresponded with the world process from Genesis to the Apocalypse, was on the one hand the *renewed spiritual human being*, the hermaphrodite of Paradise re-won in freedom. On the other hand, it was also the *renewed matter* which again carried in itself the virginal-motherly secret of cosmic life. The philosopher's stone is the symbol of the striving for this "end product."

The true Rosicrucian

Now that we have immersed ourselves to some extent in the alchemy of the Rosicrucians, we need to consider the question of whether Shakespeare had a relationship to this interesting stream in European cultural life.

Shakespeare lived at the time of the transition from the sixteenth to the seventeenth century. This period is characterized not only by a great blossoming of outer life in England, it is also very significant for the path of inner development of all mankind. For at that time something wanted to come to the surface of social life which had been prepared and had worked in secret for centuries: the impulse of the great Christian initiate who carries the name Christian Rosenkreutz.

The man Christian Rosenkreutz is not a fabrication, but a human being who exists in all reality. The story of his biography and of the way the Brotherhood came into existence, as these are reported in the *Fama Fraternitatis* by Johann Valentin Andreae, published in 1615, is firmly grounded in truth. He did not appear on the stage of outer history, but gave inspiration and impulses through personalities who had special capacities. *Among these, Shakespeare must be counted as one of the most important ones.*

I am deeply convinced that all of the many efforts to attack Shakespeare's person and his work, efforts that are continuing in our time, are related to this Rosicrucian inspiration. I am especially thinking of the underhanded way in which the first printing of his plays appeared, complete with many text corruptions, while he was still alive, as well as the stubborn doubt some people have regarding the authorship of his dramatic works. For we can hardly imagine a stream in history that has been equally misjudged, vilified, attacked, and persecuted as that of the true Rosicrucians, except perhaps the Arian Christians, Cathars, and Templars, movements that in fact had a direct or indirect relationship with the Rosicrucian impulse. This subject raises a lot of questions which in the limited framework of this study cannot be considered in detail.

What is the object of Christian Rosenkreutz' striving? And why does this so clearly come to light around 1600? In the section about alchemy I have described this striving in broad outlines. It is in service of the very loftiest goal: the Christianization of humanity and the earth. In every developmental phase of humanity, however, this striving has to adopt a form that suits that phase. For our time, the appropriate form is *natural science*, but a natural science that does not estrange human beings as free spiritual individualities from the spiritual reality of the world.

What needs to arise is a type of thinking about nature that becomes an organ of perception for the spirit in nature. This necessitates a schooling of unprejudiced observation and non-egoistic thinking; one could also say: it necessitates an elevation of observation and thinking out of the fall into sin of intellectuality. Then natural science becomes a *moral* affair, and the human being becomes able to continue the creative work of the divine powers in close association with these powers, and yet also as a *free* being.

The beginning of the seventeenth century is a critical time in evolution. Shall human beings, having emancipated themselves by the power of the intellect, take the upward path of spiritualization, or the downward path of materialism, which leads to social chaos, poisoning, and death? (See the study of *Hamlet*.)In the Middle Ages, Christian Rosenkreutz prepared the new path in the upward direction. Around 1600, the time had come for this path to be clearly demonstrated as the alternative to materialism that was then strongly announcing itself.

Here we have to take note of the fact that the human individuality, the immortal spirit or entelechy, does not live just once on earth, but continuously returns in new embodiments—reincarnation. For most people a period of a number of centuries passes between their death in one life on earth and birth in the next life. For the individuality of Christian Rosenkreutz this interval is very short. Beginning in the thirteenth century he has incarnated in every century, with the result that his inspiring power, although usually not directly recognized, is almost continually among humanity.

Early in the seventeenth century four remarkable documents were published in Germany, of which the best known are *The Chymical Wedding of Christian Rosenkreutz*, a description in imaginative pictures of an alchemical initiation, and the *Fama Fraternitatis*. They were written by a very young man, Valentin Andreae, but he was inspired by Christian Rosenkreutz himself.

Subsequently we see brotherhoods of the Rose Cross being formed in Germany, Holland, England and other European countries. Entirely peaceful and worthy of character, these brotherhoods made it their task to combat certain negative influences in the culture and to bring to realization certain positive objectives. The Rosicrucians considered as negative the influence of Arabism in philosophy and science, as well as the authority of Rome. Over against these they encouraged a development of philosophy and natural science that would not estrange the human being from the spirit, concurrent with the development of a healthy social order in Europe.

This impulse unleashed great opposition, especially from the Church. In every conceivable way the Rosicrucians were treated with suspicion, ridiculed, injured, and tortured. In Holland, for instance, the leader of the movement, the painter Torrentius, was persecuted by the Protestant preachers in the most atrocious way. However, an effective way of combating the Rosicrucians proved to be the *inversion of their actual goals*. The most evident example of this is the work of Francis Bacon, who received certain inspirations from Christian Rosenkreutz, but worked with these in an opposite sense. He inaugurated natural science in its materialistic form. In Germany the movement became the victim of the Thirty Years' War. From an external point of view, the opposing powers were victorious.

All Christian Rosenkreutz, who respects the freedom of the human personality above all else, can do is to continue to work, bearing the inversion and vilification of his impulse like a martyr, and offer his service to humanity in continuously renewed forms.

In the time of Queen Elizabeth and King James I,* the Rosicrucian impulse found a fertile soil in England; however, in this soil grew also a variety of groups that engaged in occult practices, in which seemingly the same lofty things were discussed, but which were in fact old—it was intellectualized mystery wisdom. A flourishing mishmash of astrology, alchemy, Kabala, Gnosticism, neo-Platonic, Pythagorean, hermetic, and mystic philosophies exercised the minds of the London spiritual elite. They came together in the Mermaid Tavern where the famous Sir Walter Raleigh, discoverer, philosopher, sometime poet, womanizer, and sword fighter, formed a select circle around himself of young noblemen and talented poets among which we find Spencer, Lyly, Marlowe, Kyd, Greene, Beaumont, Chapman, and Ben Johnson.

---

* A study, relevant to the present theme, concerning King James I's connections to both Shakespeare and Francis Bacon is found in R. Ramsbotham, *Who Wrote Bacon?*, Temple Lodge, 2004. [Ed.]

In this circle, Shakespeare, who had risen quickly from working in a stable to acting and writing plays, was introduced. Here he must have absorbed an inconceivable wealth of rich knowledge and wisdom. Indeed, we should not underrate the discussions on the Greek myths and mysteries, on Plato's world of ideas, the subtleties of the mysticism of courtly love, to name only a few of the subjects that occupied this circle. And yet, virtually nothing remains of these "Mermaid brothers" except stuff in libraries for students and literary connoisseurs.

But Shakespeare survived! His work alone was able to become a living leaven for posterity down to our time and far beyond it, because the ancient wisdom was rejuvenated in his soul, and he absorbed the inspiration from Christian Rosenkreutz as an impulse for the future. His "prophetic mind" was the true fertile soil for spiritual thoughts, and his gigantic collection of poetry defies corruption and denial.

Of course, other things have also survived, such as the potato and tobacco that Raleigh brought home from America. Only, these did not come out of the profound discussions in the Mermaid, and we may wonder whether these products have not brought us as much harm as the good that Shakespeare's work has brought us.

We see how Shakespeare initially reacted against the rigid teachings-in-verse of his brothers in the art. His comedy *Love's Labour's Lost* is in a certain sense a parody on the occultism of people like Chapman and Northumberland, on the "companions of the night" who wanted to attain to the higher life through strict abstinence, study, and meditation.

But on the other hand, in this early work he already reveals the maturity of his spirit. His "occultism" is nourished from a deeper spring. He knows that the development of the higher human being in us is a slow process of trial and maturation, and that a theoretical decision to renounce the world can be undone by one beguiling glance from the eyes of a woman. He has the ability to bring occult truth to life in the characters and dramatic situations of his plays. He creates dream pictures that contain more truth than daily life, but he never deviates from this ordinary daily life.

He must have been thoroughly acquainted with alchemy, not as a theory, nor as practice, but as an experience of the realities of life. Just like substances for the alchemists, human souls must have "sounded" for him. For earthly ears the music of the spheres has fallen silent, but for the adept the harmony of the stars sings in substances and souls. It is understandable that the dramatic rhythm of the five-foot iamb is now and then interrupted by the most delicious lyrical "songs." These are junctions of all that musically unfolds and flows through the entire play.

Aren't the various human souls also woven from one primal substance, just as matter appears in differentiated manifestations of the *prima materia?* This unity was lost as matter was broken into fragments on earth, but the poet/alchemist shows it to us again in the fulfillment scenes at the end of his dramas. This fulfillment is love; the original, primal substance of souls has to be love. In Shakespeare's overwhelming wealth of words there is one word that appears more than any other: Love.

At the happy endings of his comedies it is often not just one couple that reaches the fulfillment of marriage. The motif of "attachment," the birth of the higher being-in-unity is doubled, tripled. This triad in the final chord of the play is found in *A Midsummer Night's Dream, The Merchant of Venice, As You Like It,* and *The Winter's Tale.*

Why do the comedies show the alchemical element more strongly than the tragedies? It is because the comedies embody that which brings joy and fulfillment. The tragedies bring a sort of counter-alchemy, the disintegration of the human being. But there is another reason: The comedies possess the secret of humor.

Sal humor

As we have seen, the seven stages of the chymical process were: *mortificatio*–dying; *putrefactio*–decomposition; *solutio*–dissolution; *animatio*–ensoulment; *purefactio*–purification; *perfectio*–perfection; and *fixatio*–attachment.

In *As You Like It* these stages can be followed.

At the beginning a *mortificatio* mood is clearly evident; it is dominated by fratricide, initially presented in disguise in the form of the exile of the Duke, and the bad treatment of Orlando. Charles, the wrestler, in essence gets the order to be an executioner; Duke Frederick plots Orlando's demise.

There follows *putrefactio*. Lower soul tendencies such as jealousy and lust for power in Frederick and Oliver lead to disintegration. Rosalind is banished from the court; Orlando has to flee from the murderous plot of Oliver. Celia makes a sacrifice; she leaves the court to follow her niece. Adam does the same for Orlando; moreover he gives Orlando his savings.

In *solutio* everything comes into movement. Rosalind, Celia, Touchstone, Orlando, the old servant Adam— they are all separated from house and hearth, and the love that has arisen between Rosalind and Orlando flows as unfulfilled longing in the solution from which nothing can as yet precipitate.

In the Forest of Arden *animatio* begins to grow. The shepherd's life in unspoilt nature brings relief, renewal after the pains that have been suffered.

Purefactio begins with the Duke's reprimand of Orlando for the latter's impetuosity. The Duke allies himself with the inhabitants of the wood who have more or less reached the state of perfection. Music and poetry (in this case a humorous doggerel) are sounding. We should imagine the whole wood as a singing, sounding world. Even the trees are speaking love language! The purification continues in the trial Phebe has to go through: Rosalind holds up a mirror to her.

Purification transitions into *perfectio*. This culminates in the inner victory of Orlando when he sees the lioness threatening his sleeping brother. He does not repay evil with evil; he saves Oliver. This makes the turn-about of his brother possible.

Fixatio, attachment, presided over by the marriage god, coincides with a final manifestation of *perfectio*, the conversion of Duke Frederick.

One of the most salient traits of the comedy is the male impersonation by Rosalind. Travesty, the impersonation of the opposite sex, was a favorite theater motif, and we encounter it often in Shakespeare. In *The Merchant of Venice* Jessica disguises herself as a page, and Portia and Nerissa as a legal scholar and a clerk. In *Twelfth Night* we have the unforgettable Viola in a boy's suit and in *Cymbeline* the touching Imogen. This predilection for such impersonation could of course be easily explained by the fact that in Shakespeare's time all female parts were played by boys. But this outer circumstance is only secondary. The poet creates totally credible female characters, and he does not want to deny their femininity by masculine clothing. In daily life it was considered most indecent if a woman wore men's clothes. At the realistic level, impersonation of the opposite sex is a cause of misunderstanding and dramatic movement. At the psychological level, the feminine in the role of the transvestite remains decisive. At the imaginative level, however, the secret of the hermaphrodite is indicated.

In *As You Like It*, the image of the hermaphrodite in Rosalind is even stronger than in Viola or Imogen. Rosalind lets herself be courted as Ganymede by Orlando. She says that this will cure him of the pain of his love, but in the meantime she is testing his faithfulness. She raises his love up from the level of being in love with a pretty girl, and thus Orlando's love is freed from a transitory element. We recognize here the alchemical ideal of the paradisal human being shining through the seemingly childlike and airy banter of love.

Now, an objection can be made by pointing to the irrefutable fact that all of this also appears in Shakespeare's source, Lodge's *Rosalynde*, so that the alchemical elements would then not be Shakespeare's invention but Lodge's. It is true that in Lodge's story the motifs described here are indeed present, but why does it not become true soul alchemy there? Because humor is lacking! Lodge wrote his story in the so called Euphuistic style. This was an artificially delicate form of writing that was made fashionable by John Lyly's novel *Euphues*. Shakespeare replaces euphuism with the spice of humor, and only then does poetic alchemy arise.

The fact that in the genuine Rosicrucian documents, such as *The Chymical Wedding* and the *Parabola*, we can always find an element of fine, subtle humor much like the humor in folk and fairy tales, proves that humor is indispensible on the alchemical path of initiation. When we wonder to which physical processes humor is related, there is practically no direct information to be found.

In *The Chymical Wedding* we find the following passage. Brother Christian has gone on his way to attend the chymical wedding. He comes to a portal where he has to give something away. He had taken only three things with him: bread, water, and salt. He had shared the bread with a white dove. At the portal he gives the water, in return for which he receives a coin with an inscription. When he arrives at a second portal he has to give something again. He gives the salt and receives a second coin which has the inscription *S. M.* The explanation the story gives is rather obscure: *Studio Merentis*, Sal Humor, *Sponso Mittendus, Sal Mineralis, Sal Menstrualis*, meaning respectively: *To a worthy student, ...?, pledge of the bridegroom, mineral salt, purifying salt.*

Sal humor is a riddle. Is it an error in the text, since S.M. cannot mean *sal humor*? Be this as it may, perhaps the combination of *sal* and *humor* may be able to put us on the track of the humorous. Humor means fluid, liquid, and in old medicine the "humors," the juices of the body, played an important role. The dominance of one of these fluids (blood, mucus, gall, and black gall), determined the temperament, and also the mood. The fluids of the temperaments mentioned above were also seen in relation to the four elements, which were not then considered as the dead aggregates of modern science, but as the carriers of the life forces.

According to these earlier insights a person's mood or humor was an expression of the way in which the life forces worked in him or her, more or less constant in the temperament, but fluctuating in mood. In the human being the life forces work downward in the processes of the metabolism: sulphur, combustion; they work upward in the nerve-sense system where an extremely fine salt formation occurs. Too much salt formation would rigidify the organism and cause death; the life-carrying humors must therefore constantly dissolve and create warmth.

Sal humor is then the force needed to permeate the crystal-clear with warm life; and isn't that the essence of humor, of the humorous? In genuine humor lives the salt of wisdom, but also the warmth of the dissolving love element. Only, humor is not the *lofty* connection of wisdom, love, and the warmth of sacrifice; it is a subtle *shift* from the lofty to the absurd. The Frenchman says: "*Du sublime au ridicule, ce n'est qu'un pas*" (From the sublime to the ridiculous is but a step), a saying by Napoleon who, by the way, did not excel in humor.

A plant is virtually never humorous; at best we can speak of a funny little flower, or see something humorous in the contortions of tree roots and gnarled branches. An animal much more often evokes a humorous mood, although of course animals do not consciously produce humor. The fact that humor does have something to do with animals but hardly ever with plants means that the humorous is not only related to the humors and life forces but also to what is ensouled. For in contrast with the plant, the animal possesses awareness, feeling—it is ensouled therefore.

Now, the ensouled always carries an element of desire in itself. A plant, without desire, is perfectly pure in its manifestation of life. In the animal, desire does not yet lie in the sphere of morality because the animal possesses no conscious morality, but as an image of the impure in desire we are justified in using the animal-like. When however this impure element, this lowness, is shifted a little it can make us laugh. The salt of humor is therefore also *sal menstrualis*, salt of purification.

Humor arises both when the higher and when the lower is shifted a little. In both cases something dissolves and something crystallizes. The mysterious power of humor is a chymical paradox that apparently has its necessary task in the great work of becoming perfect.

The jester is not the only one who carries this power in the comedy; actually, his humor tends to be somewhat on the intellectual side. The two nieces are at least as humorous as he, and we should also not overlook the bitter humor of Jaques. The poet permeates the entire process of his comedy with humor, and it is this element that makes it into soul alchemy.

The Forest of Arden, the "other" place, the realm of fulfillment, is not the strict world of renunciation and hidden temple mysticism; it is the world of nature and the soul that lies open to everyone's gaze, the world of nature in the soul and of the soul in nature. Whether our gaze is able to behold the mystery in this world depends on our inner preparation. May this study be a contribution to this preparation, so that we will see the incomparable work of art of *As You Like It*, with new eyes and hear it with new ears.

6

THE WINTER'S TALE

Resurrection of the Soul

The motif of resurrection

The Winter's Tale, together with *Pericles, Cymbeline*, and *The Tempest*, belongs to the last group of stage plays Shakespeare wrote. The subject of this romantic comedy, which begins in a dark and wild mood like a tragedy, is derived from a story in prose by Robert Greene, an older contemporary of Shakespeare. In that story, *Pandosto, the Triumph of Time* (later entitled *Dorastus and Fawnia*), Queen Bellaria—Shakespeare's Hermione—dies due to the injustice she suffers. Shakespeare changes this: Queen Hermione does not really die. For sixteen years she lives in seclusion, thought by her repentant husband to be dead, until at the end of the play she is "brought back to life."

It is of course no coincidence that both in *The Winter's Tale* and in *Pericles* and *Cymbeline* the same motif is central. In *The Tempest* too we find images of resurrection when Prospero makes himself known to his erstwhile enemies who thought they had killed him, and when Prince Ferdinand, playing chess with Miranda in Prospero's cave, is shown to the astonished eyes of Alonso and his companions.

The theme of the "resurrection from death" is already prepared in *Much Ado about Nothing*, an earlier comedy in which, as in *The Winter's Tale*, a woman seemingly per-ishes due to slander but is later restored to honor and happiness as if raised from the dead. Between *Much Ado about Nothing* and *The Winter's Tale* lie all the great trag-edies in which death is the dark and irrevocable end.

In the chapter on *Hamlet* it has been pointed out that in *Hamlet, Othello,* and *King Lear* the principal female fig-ure loses her life because her breath is cut off. In the realm of imagination this is a picture of the suffocation of the anima, the soul. The principal female figures in the final creative period of the poet, Thaisa (*Pericles*), Imogen (*Cymbeline*), and Hermione (*The Winter's Tale*) similarly represent the soul element, but here they go through death to new life.

While Shakespeare seems to have felt the need in his middle period to put the suffocation of the soul on the stage repeatedly—witness Ophelia's purity besmirched by suicide in insanity, Desdemona by diabolical jealousy, and Cordelia by hatred—in his last dramas he shows how purity triumphs, how the soul as immortal being vanquishes death and darkness.

In this regard, the tragedy of *Romeo and Juliet* is also a remarkable herald of the later apotheosis of resurrec-tion. In the plan of Brother Lawrence, Juliet, who was already married but then immediately after the wedding night separated from her husband, had to go through a "death sleep" in order to become forever united with her beloved. Because of the fatal course of events the plan goes awry; the messenger from Verona is unable to reach Romeo in time. The latter finds his Juliet lying in the family tomb of the Capulets and, imagining her dead, he takes his own life. Juliet then awakens "from her death" only to die a real death. The apotheosis of the soul is here presented in the certainty that the "star-crossed lovers" are united in death. And this eternal union is cemented on earth by the reconciliation of the two hostile families of the Capulets and Montagues.

Thus the motif of death and resurrection pervades the entire work of Shakespeare; it goes through metamorphoses, goes into hiding, only to reappear in greater clarity. There where death is shown as the irrevocable end the question of resurrection sounds the more strongly, as in *Hamlet* where the "place of the skull" in Elsinore is a shuddering counter-image of Golgotha.

Inevitably, the great soul alchemist becomes the great poet of resurrection, the Christian poet *par excellence*. But Shakespeare's Christianity is not the Christianity of a dogmatic church. It is not the Catholic or Protestant clerics he puts on the stage who represent the Christian element, but rather the worldly figures. Nowhere does he dare to go further in this regard than in *Measure for Measure*, in which a worldly prince, albeit disguised as a monk, bestows absolution on someone awaiting execution in prison. Not surprisingly, the Roman Catholic Church placed this play on the index.

Shakespeare's Christianity is the Christianity of an initiate who brings the eternal truth of the gospels to us in dramatic pictures, without a word of doctrine—all is in images. In this regard *The Winter's Tale* forms a real culminating-point, just as in poetic respects and as a drama it belongs to the most beautiful things Shakespeare has written.

The story

Act I

Polyxenes, King of Bohemia, is staying with Leontes, King of Sicily, as his guest. When he wants to return to Bohemia, Leontes tries to convince him to stay a while longer. Queen Hermione carries the day in a courtly but cordial and graceful competition: Polyxenes agrees to stay another week in Sicily. Leontes is angry; he thinks the persuasiveness of his spouse was too ardent to be innocent. He looks askance at Polyxenes and Hermione who have taken each other's hand in an intimate and friendly conversation.

In the meantime, Leontes speaks partly to himself, partly to his little son Mamillius who cannot understand the inflated jealousy and the somewhat rough caresses of his father. Hermione and Polyxenes notice that Leontes is disturbed, but the latter evades their question by talking about his youth, joking with Mamillius, and asking about Polyxenes' little son. Hermione and Polyxenes go into the garden and, alone with the boy, Leontes indulges in his all-consuming jealousy.

Camillo, a Sicilian nobleman, enters and Leontes, ensnared ever deeper in his disastrous suspicion, shares it with Camillo. Indignantly the nobleman rejects the blame that is thus thrown on his queen, but Leontes rages on and on. He urges Camillo to mix poison into Polyxenes' wine. Camillo calls Leontes' suspicions a delusion, an illness, but in the end he obeys his lord. He will poison Polyxenes but demands that the queen will go scot-free. Leontes agrees and leaves.

Camillo expresses his despair regarding the situation in which he finds himself. He must obey his king, but he does not want to be the murderer of a king. He decides to flee from the Sicilian court. Polyxenes enters and expresses his surprise at the coldness with which Leontes has just now responded to him. Camillo does not want to say anything at first, but then he tells him everything. He adjures Polyxenes not to try to prove his innocence, because he knows that his king will not listen to reason. Polyxenes joins Camillo in his decision to leave the country as soon as possible. They will go together.

Act II

A lady-in-waiting tells Mamillius that his mother, Hermione, is expecting a baby. Hermione then calls him to tell her a story. In a whisper he begins: "There was a man ... dwelt by a churchyard."

Leontes comes in accompanied by courtiers who have told him that Polyxenes has left the country posthaste together with Camillo. The king sees this as a confirmation of his suspicions and in a rage he first chases Mamillius away from his mother and then accuses Hermione of adultery and conspiracy with Camillo against his life. Full of dignity and warmth, the noble queen professes her innocence. Leontes does not believe her and has her locked up in the dungeon. The courtiers, including a certain Antigonus, attempt in vain to change Leontes' mind. Ranting and raving he shuts them up. To Antigonus's words that he should surely have verified things before spreading them abroad Leontes replies that he has sent two noblemen to the oracle of Apollo, so as to receive a divine judgment on the affair.

Paulina, Antigonus's wife, visits Hermione in the dungeon. She is not admitted but learns that Hermione has given birth to a baby daughter. She offers to go to the king with the little child in order to plead Hermione's case with great force. This happens, but the noble and courageous Paulina merely aggravates his blind rage. He yells at her and her husband that he is not the father but Polyxenes, and in the end he even orders the unhappy Antigonus to throw the child into the fire.

He then mitigates this horrible sentence when his courtiers swear that Antigonus in no way encouraged Paulina to come to him with the child, which is what Leontes was assuming. The gentler sentence, however, is no less radical: Antigonus must take the baby away to a distant place and leave it behind so that it will perish.

Antigonus swears to do this. A messenger comes in with the report that the envoys to the oracle have returned.

Act III

Cleomenes and Dion, returned from Delphi, are speaking together about the solemn and wondrous impression the oracle has made on them. They hope that the judgment, which is written on a sealed scroll, will prove the innocence of the queen.

Hermione has to appear in court. The accusation is read. Again she professes her innocence. Leontes turns to her full of abuse and scorn and threatens her with the due reward for her deeds. Hermione says that death can only be welcome after all she has suffered and after the loss of Leontes' respect and love. But to save her honor she asks to hear the divine judgment of Apollo.

The envoys are shown in; an official reads the oracle, which plainly states that Hermione, Polyxenes and Camillo are innocent; that Leontes is a jealous tyrant; that the baby was born in all honor and decency, and that the king will die without an heir if the child that is lost is not found. Everyone praises Apollo, but Leontes in his foolhardiness denies the truth of the divine judgment.

At that moment a servant reports that Mamillius, who had been suffering from a lingering disease ever since the accusation of his mother, has died. Hermione faints and is carried away. Leontes, cured of his rage by this blow of fate, implores Apollo to forgive his blasphemy. He admits the innocence of his wife, of Camillo and Polyxenes, and accuses himself.

With loud lamentations Paulina comes in with the news that the queen has died. She does not spare Leontes in her wild accusations, but the latter deems this justified. Paulina is moved by his repentance; she asks for forgiveness for her hard words. Leontes wants her to take him to his dead wife and child.

On the coast of Bohemia, Antigonus has landed with the little princess. An awful storm is threatening, but he takes the time to put the poor baby carefully down, wrapped in a mantle of Hermione. Full of feeling he tells the pitiful little creature that her mother appeared to him in a dream and told him to call the child Perdita, the lost one, and to leave it on the coast of Bohemia. Although he had to do this in obedience to his king, he will because of this ignoble deed never see his Paulina again. The dream comes true: shortly after this a wild bear attacks and devours him.

An old shepherd appears during the now breaking storm, grumbling at his son who went hunting in this awful weather. He finds the baby and is very glad. His son (the text has: "clown") comes to him at the same moment, full of two amazing scenes he has seen: the wrecking of a ship and the death of an old man by a bear.

Together they examine the valuables of the poor baby and they decide to take the child with them. A purse with gold was lying by the baby. "It is a happy day, my boy," says the old shepherd, " and therefore we want to do good things today."

Act IV

Time, an allegorical person, tells us that sixteen years have passed.

In his repentance, Leontes has turned away from the world. Perdita has grown into a beautiful young shepherd girl with whom Florizel, crown prince of Bohemia, has fallen in love. Polyxenes expresses his uneasiness to Camillo in regard to Florizel, because he is so often not at home. Camillo, who has asked Polyxenes for permission to return to Sicily, promises to accompany Polyxenes to a shepherd's family where it is said that there is a very pretty daughter, who is probably the magnet that draws Florizel away from his princely duties.

We become acquainted with Autolycus—"a rogue"—who, merrily singing, introduces himself as a lusty scoundrel and proceeds to prove this right away by relieving the silly "clown" of his purse. The latter was on his way to buy things for the sheep-shearing festival in which his pretty sister will be queen. At the beginning of the feast we see Florizel and the enchanting Perdita. Their love is strong, but the girl is afraid that the great distance between the prince and her will lead to problems, since she is but a simple shepherd's daughter. But Florizel refuses to listen; he is firmly determined to marry her.

The guests arrive, including Polyxenes and Camillo in disguise. They are greeted in the most charming manner by Perdita. The shepherds and shepherdesses are dancing when a servant announces the arrival of a pedlar. It is the sly Autolycus who charges high prices for his songs and party junk. A little quarrel arises between Mopsa and Dorcas who are both trying to be noticed by the rogue.

After some more festive songs and fun, such as a dance of twelve shepherds dressed up as satyrs, Polyxenes has the opportunity to separate the two lovers. When Florizel in front of the two unknown gentlemen says that he wants to be engaged to Perdita, Polyxenes throws back his hood and turns into the strict king who calls his son to order. With an angry snarl at the old shepherd, and threatening the girl with terrible punishment if she continues to try to win the prince, Polyxenes leaves.

The whining old shepherd is so frightened that it never dawns on him to reveal the secret of his beautiful "daughter." Florizel is unwavering in his decision to wed Perdita. A ship is ready to take them to another place. Camillo, who had stayed behind when Polyxenes left, suggests to Florizel and his shepherdess to flee to Sicily, where he may expect a favorable reception and support from Leontes. The clever councilor sees an opportunity in this to return to his country himself. For he intends to betray the flight of the young people to the king and convince him to pursue them. In this way, Camillo will then be able to make his longed-for return to Sicily.

Autolycus, who appears loudly boasting of his pickpocketing successes, is going to play a role in the flight: he has to exchange clothes with Florizel. The rogue smells his profit, wants to report everything to the king, but then runs into the old shepherd and his son. These want to make a confession to the king as to the events around the supposed shepherd's daughter. They are bringing a box in which they have put the valuables they had found with the little foundling.

Autolycus passes himself off as a courtier, makes the simple duo terribly afraid, but promises to help them, in return for which they give him their gold. He says he will bring them on board the ship on which the king is already embarked. But he points them to Florizel's ship, because he thinks he can in this way do his former master, the prince, a favor which, of course, will bring him another reward.

Act V

In Sicily, Cleomenes is speaking with King Leontes. He is trying to convince the king that after all those years of repentance, he has paid his due. Leontes denies this, and Paulina supports him. By speaking of Hermione she keeps the soul wound of Leontes open. Cleomenes is one of those who want the king to remarry. Paulina ardently disagrees and reminds them of the judgment of the oracle; she makes Leontes swear that he will never remarry without her consent. The king swears to this. "That shall be," says Paulina, "when your first queen's again in breath; never till then."

A nobleman comes in to report the arrival of Prince Florizel and his spouse. He profusely praises the beauty of the girl. The young pair is shown in and Leontes receives them graciously. He is touched by the brotherly message Florizel brings from his father—on the advice of Camillo.

Suddenly, however, the report arrives that Polyxenes has himself landed in Sicily; he greets Leontes with the request to arrest his son Florizel who has fled with a shepherd's daughter. He is on his way to the court, but has run into the old father and brother of the fake princess who are now being interrogated by Camillo. Leontes promises to go and meet Polyxenes in order to plead for Florizel and his beauty.

The events that follow now are not enacted on stage, but are related by noblemen to Autolycus who has come along to Sicily. It is a heart-rending story of surprise and jubilating joy. The packet of Perdita has been opened and has proven without a shadow of doubt that Perdita is the long lost daughter of Hermione and Leontes. Everyone, also the old shepherd and his son, is overjoyed.

Perdita, deeply touched by the story of her mother's death, now wants to see the statue that has just been finished in Paulina's house, and of which it is said that it is a miraculously true image of the unfortunate queen.

Before we are led to the statue we meet two newly-baked noblemen: the ennobled shepherd and his son. They have become so noble that they forgive the scoundrel Autolycus who apologizes for all the trouble he has caused them, on condition that he will improve his behavior from now on and pull himself together. He promises to do his best.

Everyone now comes together in Paulina's house. They are shown the statue of Hermione. Deeply touched, Leontes wants to touch it. Paulina prevents this, but as by magic she lets the statue step out of its niche. The living Hermione is embraced by Leontes. She does not speak until she implores the gods' blessings on her daughter who is kneeling before her. The hope given by the oracle that the child could be saved has kept her alive. After Paulina had initially taken the deep faint of the queen for death and had reported this to Leontes, it turned out that Hermione's life had not in fact left her. In her wisdom, however, Paulina pretended that she had died. Trusting in the oracle, she kept Hermione hidden all those years.

The child was found; the happy reunion can take place. Only old Antigonus, Paulina's husband, does not return. Paulina wants, as an "old turtle," to find "some wither'd bough, and there my mate, that's never to be found again, lament till I am lost." But Leontes leads her to faithful Camillo in whom she will find a worthy spouse. And now everyone is invited to go

...where we may leisurely
Each one demand, and answer to his part
Perform'd in this wide gap of time, since first
We were dissever'd: hastily lead away! [5.3]

Kings and shepherds

Shakespeare followed the story by Robert Greene quite faithfully in the first three acts; he only changed the names of the principal characters and swapped the realms of Leontes and Polyxenes: Sicily became the background of the dark drama of jealousy, and Bohemia became Polyxenes kingdom where the fourth act takes place, which is entirely Shakespeare's own composition. With the turn of the story to the radiant shepherds' episode, and thus also to the happy ending, Shakespeare lifted the whole story up far above the tragic-romantic sphere that characterizes literary creations of this genre.

Moreover, he gave the motif of resurrection from death a most interesting background by letting the contrast

Sicily-Bohemia coincide with the polarity of *kings and shepherds*—Sicily, the realm where royal power and royal wisdom degenerate into tyranny and delusion; Bohemia, the realm of flourishing shepherd love, flanked by simpleness and knavery. For the happy outcome it is necessary that the kingly element and the shepherd element be connected.

Perdita, the lost royal child, grows up as a shepherdess, and only when her royal identity has been discovered can her mother, Hermione, return to life and can Leontes be redeemed from his doom.

Although the contrast between the realm of the high-born and that of the lowly also occurs elsewhere in Shakespeare's work, only in *The Winter's Tale* does it receive its full archetypal significance because here it is placed in relation to the *birth of a child*. We are reminded of the birth stories in the gospels of St. Matthew and St. Luke, of the wise kings from the East and the simple shepherds around Bethlehem.

The atmosphere of these two stories is very different. According to St. Matthew, the Jesus child, who is descended from David in the royal line, is sought, found and adored by kings. Facing these good kings stands the evil King Herod. He wants to find the child in order to kill it. The joyful event is overshadowed by darkness and malevolence.

In the sphere of kings the darkness is mixed into the light; the darkness wants to destroy the light; there is conflict, tension and tragedy. This is also the case in fairy tales, sagas, and in history. Wisdom and power, the divine attributes of kingship, may degenerate into diabolical counter-images. We clearly see this in Leontes, whose wisdom is perverted by insane jealousy. The epitome of his folly has to be his rejection of the divine oracle that absolved Hermione of all guilt.

He also abuses his power in many ways. He orders Camillo to poison his royal guest Polyxenes. He silences his courtiers when they dare speak against his suspicions and rough treatment of Hermione. He wants to have the newly born child killed and orders Antigonus to leave it somewhere to die. In every "evil" king we see manifested the archetypal picture of *the* evil king, Herod. In Leontes this is totally clear: he thinks he is killing a foreign royal child, but in reality he kills, indirectly, his son Mamillius. And does not the story of Herod tell that he had his own son killed?

In the birth story according to St. Luke, the element of darkness is not there. At best we might feel it in the phrase "because there was no room for them in the inn." The tradition of the birth plays of the Middle Ages has therefore produced a number of unfriendly innkeepers who represent a hostile world. The child that is sought by the pious shepherds is descended from David in the priestly line of Nathan. The apocryphal legends that were woven around this child in the course of time all speak of its loveliness, its compassion. We are here in the sphere of "wonder," of paradisal innocence and purity.

The shepherds who find little Perdita are no shepherds of Bethlehem, but here too we see compassion and simplicity sketched with humor, the sphere of wonder. The coastal area of Bohemia, where sixteen years later the delightful shepherds' festival is enacted, shines in the light of a wealth of flowers, paradisal purity and unwavering love. The poet does put the element of evil into the mix: the wrathful king who threatens the innocent girl with the most cruel punishment; but in a certain sense this anger is justified in the light of a possible misalliance of his son. And then we have the malevolence of Autolycus, but it is that of a rogue, relatively innocent therefore. Moreover, the sly freebooter and pickpocket has a positive share in the happy outcome: involuntarily he contributes to the ennoblement of his simple victims, the old shepherd and his son.

Traditional Christianity has lost the secret of the polarity of kings and shepherds in connection with the birth of Jesus. No one notices the characteristic differences between the stories of St. Matthew and St. Luke anymore; they are merely regarded as variations of one and the same event. The difference between the "royal" genealogy in St. Matthew and the "shepherdly" genealogy in St. Luke is disregarded or, mark you, declared to be an error—as if an error would be possible in something of that importance! But this is not the place to elaborate on the insight into the mystery of the birth of Jesus offered by modern spiritual science.*

With regard to the polarity of kings versus shepherds a few remarks will have to suffice which are important in relation to our subject. Here again we enter a curious territory in which archetypal images coincide with outer reality, this time not in a geographical sense such as in the biblical landscapes of Judea and Galilee (see *As You Like It*), but in an historical sense.

There have always been certain streams that work in human evolution. One of these could be called the kingly stream, another the shepherds' or priestly stream; these two relate to each other as a polarity. They can be regarded as "columns" of humanity that have a carrying role in history.

The kings, bearers of power and wisdom, represent the human being as ruler of the earthly world. Originally they received their knowledge not from the earth, but from the world of the stars. They were able to spell the cosmic signs in heaven as revelations of divine beings,

* See Rudolf Steiner, *According to Luke*, CW 114, SteinerBooks; and Emil Bock, *The Childhood of Jesus*, Floris Books.

and could thus understand and rule the earthly world. This form of kingship, however, was gradually lost. The Wise Men from the East were the last representatives of this old astrological knowledge. It enabled them to perceive the star of Jesus and interpret it in the right way.

The shepherds, bearers of piety and readiness to sacrifice, represent the human being as servant of the heavenly world. They had no outer knowledge, but their loving hearts bestowed on them the capacity to receive spiritual revelations at certain moments. They were children of the earth, but did not rule the earth. They were sovereign in the world of the heart.

In history, and in fairy tales and legends we often see that a high point of humanness is reached when the kingly and the shepherdly are united. Examples are David, the shepherd boy, who becomes the greatest king of Israel; and Prince Siddharta, son of an Indian king, who became the great soul shepherd Buddha. When Dante is at the top of the Mountain of Purgatory, his spiritual guide Virgil places on his head the crowns of both the Pope (shepherd) and the emperor.

The highest revelation of this connection between the streams of the kings and the shepherds is realized in Jesus of Nazareth whose double human nature hides a deep mystery. This most wise, loving, royal-priestly human being became in the Baptism in the Jordan in his thirtieth year the bearer of the Christ Spirit that descended from the Most High God. By his incarnation, Christ sets the seal on the connection of the kingly with the shepherds' stream, both of which had worked since time immemorial in preparation for the descent of the Redeemer, the true *representative of humanity*.

We must therefore make a distinction between the paradisal element of the shepherd in the *human being* Jesus and the pure divine element of the Christ Being.

There exists much misunderstanding in this regard, which is nourished by ecclesiastical tradition, where Jesus and the Christ Being are usually considered as one and the same. By the incarnation of the divine being, human beings, in their original nature both king and shepherd, could be redeemed from the fall into matter. The gospels say: the Son of Man is lifted up. This occurs by the mystery of death and resurrection.

Rudolf Steiner points out that in Christian times the shepherds' and royal streams continue in a certain form. They cross over. The "shepherds," who formerly lived in the inner world of the heart, in today's culture direct their attention to the outside. They are the observers of nature, such as Leeuwenhoek, Haeckel, and many other researchers.

The kingly stream is in modern times represented by abstract-mathematical thinkers, such as Kepler, Newton, Einstein. These people no longer live like the former kings with spiritual revelations from the outer world of the cosmos, but in their inner web of thought. The modern "kings" are threatened by the danger of abstract, therefore dead spirituality; the "shepherds" by the danger of spiritless sensory perception. The combination of these can be recognized in today's materialism.

These dangers can also be seen in a different light. The "kingly" element may harbor something deadly, while the "shepherd" element may lead to thoughtlessness, silliness. Out of the kingly sphere abstract-mechanistic thoughts work with suggestive power, and have engendered a world picture for us in which the soul can no longer truly live. In the shepherd sphere there is a tendency to banality in thinking, to a desire to live purely in natural phenomena, as a result of which the soul loses its bearings.

In *The Winter's Tale* we do not yet encounter the

"kings" and "shepherds" of modern culture; Shakespeare still puts real kings and shepherds on the stage. But the *images* of the drama are perfectly obvious: Leontes exudes something deadly. It is directed against the virtuous mother with her child; it destroys the male heir (the spirit element of the future); it denies the divine wisdom of Apollo. Leontes becomes "the man who dwelt by a churchyard," who can only be spoken of in whispers.

The shepherds of Bohemia are kindhearted, but also almost outrageous in their silliness. It is therefore easy for the rogue Autolycus to take advantage of them when he appears at the festival with his questionable merchandise. He only carries things that please ear and eye by their deceptive outer appearance. Whoever buys them not only finds out that he bought worthless stuff, but after the party he also notices that his purse is gone.

When the disguised King Polyxenes reproaches Prince Florizel for not buying the pedlar's entire stock of knick-knacks for his beloved, the young man replies:

> Old sir, I know
> She prizes not such trifles as these are:
> The gifts she looks from me are pack'd and lock'd
> Up in my heart, which I have given already,
> But not deliver'd. [4.3]

Florizel does not lose his bearings because he sees through the external appearance, just like Bassanio in *The Merchant of Venice*, and he knows that his Perdita, whom he calls Flora, the divine being of nature, can only be won with gifts from his heart.

Shakespeare, who as child of nature had many shepherd-like traits, devoted a large part of his works to the problem of the king. When he came to London from Stratford-on-Avon, he first served in a shepherd-like situation: he cared for the horses of the prominent spectators at the theater. As an actor and playwright, he was in the service of kings, but his royal spirit recognized the decline of the outer sacred aspect of kingship. His dramas about kings not only reflect English history, they are also reminders, gentle warnings by an initiated Bard addressed to his royal masters.

He points to inner royalty. This refers not just to actual kings, but it has to be developed and go through catharsis in each human being. Thus the royal persons in his last dramas, such as Pericles and Leontes, do not so much go through trials related to their outer positions as kings, such as the Richards and the Henrys, but they wrestle with general human weaknesses, vices and trials. In Leontes it is the overwhelming rage of jealousy that makes him commit inhuman deeds. Did Shakespeare himself perhaps labor under the all-consuming power of this vice?

Othello, Posthumus, and Leontes stand before us as monumental figures of jealousy. In Othello, darkness personified in diabolical Iago, is still victorious. Posthumus in *Cymbeline* is also the victim of malevolence: Iachimo who pours the poison of jealousy into him. It is the noble and touching Imogen who brings the change to the good and forgives her husband for all the suffering he has caused her. Leontes, who carries Iago-Iachimo in himself, experiences a complete change: the cure, the victory of the light, takes place *in him*.

The inner destruction that jealousy can work in the soul was familiar to Shakespeare, and he has depicted it like no other artist. What he himself may have lived through and purified we can only surmise. The poet himself remains in the shadows; his mighty dramatic figures stand in the light. But who would not believe that this light, out of the overshadowed heart of the poet, was born by the power of resurrection?

It is of deep significance that Leontes' turn-about strikes like a lightning bolt at the report of the death of Mamillius. This leads us to another great motif in *The Winter's Tale*: the child.

The child

In stirring pictures, the tragedy of Macbeth places the child before our eyes: the child as the victim of the power of evil and the victorious child with the Tree of Life. Macduff's little son fall at the hands of murderers; the royal child Malcolm triumphs over the dark forces of Macbeth. But, although Malcolm and Macduff, representatives of the spiritual power of the child, are able to destroy the evil tyrant, they cannot save him. They liberate the world from an evil, but do not redeem the evil.

In *The Winter's Tale* there is also a child that dies and a "lost" child that returns to bring redemption. Mamillius dies due to the blind tyranny of his father, but his death brings a sudden change in the soul of Leontes. His death is as an expiatory sacrifice through which the diabolical force disappears as suddenly as it had appeared. Perdita, the lost child, completes the redemption of the king. Her return to Sicily signifies the total reconciliation with the oracle, making the resurrection of Hermione possible.

Macduff, the prematurely born, is motivated by revenge. He consciously seeks and faces his enemy; he finds him during the battle, guided by the spirits of his murdered wife and children. Perdita, whose birth also occurs prematurely and in an unusual manner (in the dungeon), is motivated by love. She goes to Leontes as to someone unknown, unconscious of the redemption she will bring him. She is guided by the spirit of her dead brother and by the spirit of her mother who, although she is not dead, has turned away from the earth.

The grandiose nature of Shakespeare lies not only in what is perceptible to the eye and ear in each separate play, but most of all in that which lives invisibly and inaudibly in the metamorphoses of the motifs in his entire dramatic work. We are on the track of his own spiritual development, when we immerse ourselves in the metamorphosis of the child motif moving from the tragedy *Macbeth* to the comedy *The Winter's Tale*.

Why does the tragedy show the imagination of a male child with the Tree of Life from Paradise, and the *Tale* a female child as the bearer of paradisal purity? In *Macbeth* Shakespeare touches on the mystery of the spirit, in *The Winter's Tale* on the mystery of the soul. In *Macbeth* reigns the spiritual severity of justice. We are reminded of the great battle at the end of the world. Behind Malcolm and Macduff looms the apocalyptic Horseman who vanquishes the hosts of the Beast and the kings of the earth (Rev. 19). In *The Winter's Tale* lives the soul mildness of mercy. There is suffering and oppression but also liberation and joy. Behind Hermione and Perdita looms the picture of the Apocalyptic Woman (Rev. 12). Here too there is severity and justice; they sound from the lashing words of Paulina, but it is justice clothed in the soul mantle of a woman. Paulina is touched to compassion by Leontes' repentance.

While the themes of death and resurrection, kings and shepherds, and the child may indicate a deep Christian inspiration at work in Shakespeare, we will see that in his *Tale* Greek mystery wisdom is also to be found. The fact that he connects this wisdom with the Christian element, as this was also shown in other plays, proves that the separation the Church created between pagans and Christians does not exist for him. He demonstrates that true Christianity is the fulfillment and not the destruction of the ancient mysteries.

In this regard, and in many other regards as well, Shakespeare is akin to the painter Raphael. The latter's mighty frescoes in the Vatican—the *Parnassus*, the *Disputa* and the so-called *School of Athens*—similarly bring to expression the connection of paganism and Christianity. The extent to which certain interests in the Church wanted to deny and obliterate this connection is evident from the fact that the real subject of the *School of Athens*, which is the encounter of the Greek initiate Dionysius with the Christian initiate Paul, was falsified. The words *Timeo* and *Etica* which can be read on the books held by the two central figures create the impression that the older person is Plato and the younger one Aristotle. However, these words were not painted there by Raphael.* The connection of paganism with Christianity has a great deal to do with Paul, the apostle to the pagans, so it is significant that the name given to the key figure in *The Winter's Tale* is Paulina.

The goddesses of Eleusis

In her book *Shakespeare's Flowering of the Spirit*, Margaret Bennell refers to the mysteries of Eleusis in relation to *The Winter's Tale*. For instance, she explains in the light of this relationship the exchange of Sicily and Bohemia, as compared with Greene's *Pandosto*, and her arguments are noteworthy. Of old, Sicily is a place where strong forces work out of the earth into the human being who enters the island. These tellurian forces are of a dark, fiery nature, which the Greek myth has expressed in the shackling of the fire-breathing giants under Mount Etna by heavenly Zeus. Sicily is also the abode of the one-eyed Cyclopes, similarly a sinister and impetuous sort of race.

---

* Hermann Grimm, *Raphael*.

In the Middle Ages, Caltabellotta in Sicily was considered to be the black-magical center from which the magician Klingsor directed his anti-Grail activities with strong, demonic passions which the powerful tellurian forces there stirred up. In our time Sicily is known as the home of the Mafia.

The sinister storm of jealousy that, according to the play, attacks Leontes very suddenly could be caused by these negative forces in Sicily. By contrast, the Greeks considered Sicily as the island of Persephone, to whose influence they ascribed the lush, fruitful vegetation of the place. From here she was abducted by Hades, the god of the underworld. That Shakespeare brought the beautiful and lovely Perdita in connection with Persephone (Proserpina to the Romans) is evident from the text:

... O Proserpina,
For the flowers now, that, frighted, thou let'st fall
From Dis's waggon! [4.4]

Perdita invokes Proserpina and thus expresses her own inner being, says Margaret Bennell. She too was violently snatched from Sicily, leaving a grieving mother behind; when she returns, she too brings new spring flowers in the withered, wintry landscape. The connection of mother and daughter in *The Winter's Tale* with the goddesses of Eleusis becomes even more convincing when we realize that Persephone's mother, Demeter, was worshipped in the Sicilian city of Syracuse under the name of Hermione. In the mystery center of Eleusis near Athens, the aspirants were shown every year the abduction of Persephone in the form of a drama. The return of Persephone, the reunion with her mother Demeter and the mystical connection with the god Dionysus formed the higher stages of the initiation in Eleusis. The French author Edouard Schuré (1841-1929) has reconstructed this "archetypal drama of Eleusis," from which all Greek theater came forth, in a remarkable way, but much of its content had of course been known for a very long time as the myth of Persephone, also in Shakespeare's day.

In my opinion, however, Margaret Bennell makes the connection between *The Winter's Tale* and the Eleusinian mystery dramas, and their place in the initiation process, a little too easily. There are traits in Shakespeare's play which, when viewed at the imaginative level, deviate strongly from the Persephone myth. The indication Antigonus receives from Hermione in a dream to take the baby to the coast of Bohemia runs counter to the total ignorance of Demeter as to the whereabouts of her lost daughter. The objection can be made that the indication in the dream was probably not given consciously by Hermione, but that a divine power was working through her. But from the point of view of mythology, there is an essential difference with the Eleusinian story.

Then the abduction itself. Persephone is a beautiful, flourishing virgin who is taken by sinister Hades to the underworld, where she leads a grievous life as queen of the realm of the dead. Baby Perdita is not abducted by the evil one and taken to his somber realm, but expelled by the evil one (in this case her father) from his kingdom, and lands in a lovely, blooming shepherds' place where she will later, when she has grown into a beautiful virgin, find her prince. Thus the interesting exposition by Margaret Bennell does not fully add up. In my opinion, she has given too much credence to the views of Paul Arnold who, in his otherwise most interesting book *L'ésotérisme de Shakespeare* connects *The Winter's Tale* so closely with the Persephone myth, that he even wants to recognize the Hades figure in that of Autolycus. He sees both as seducers and contaminators of soul purity. I am afraid that Arnold is off the mark here.

Rushing down on the trail of Eleusis, he forgets that

we are in the realm of the shepherds, and that in the "meeting of the gods," as Florizel calls the festival, the shepherd god Hermes or Mercury, who was also the god of thieves, must not be wanting. Autolycus introduces himself emphatically as a representative of Mercury.

The only thing that is indeed in agreement with the Eleusinian myth is the picture of the two-in-one of mother and daughter, their cruel separation, and their happy reunion after they have passed through trials. The person of Hermione does indeed show a resemblance with the earth goddess Demeter: her noble stature, her chastity, her grief; but the difference between queen and goddess is at least as big as the likeness.

If Shakespeare consciously or unconsciously worked an Eleusinian element into his *Tale*, we find this not so much in the repetition of mythological images as in the Greek approach to the riddle of the human soul. The Greeks saw in the duo Demeter-Persephone not exclusively the divine forces of blossoming and withering nature. They knew that the mother goddess Demeter, the regent of the nature world, was originally also the guardian of moral-spiritual forces. In very ancient times, natural law and moral law were not yet separate. Human beings still lived with their inner world turned to the outer. Soul was nature; nature was ensouled.

Persephone represented the inner power in human beings that still enabled them to behold the unity of the world of nature with the spirit world; she was the representative of the pre-reflective, clairvoyant consciousness which has often been mentioned in these studies. For the Greek, such a representative was not only a capacity of the soul, but also a concrete, spiritual being, a goddess. As in the course of time human beings lived gradually more deeply in the earthliness of their material bodies (the dark underworld of Hades), they lost the goddess Persephone and, with her, the cosmic spirit of nature, Demeter. In the mysteries, however, it was still possible to maintain that connection.

In popular religion the reunion of Persephone with Demeter was expressed in the annual alternation of the withering and blossoming of nature. For the initiate the Persephone myth was not only a nature myth but just as much a myth of the human soul. After Shakespeare had shown the downfall of the "anima" in his tragedies, in his last dramas he wishes to express the resurrection of the soul. For this he chooses in *Pericles* and *The Winter's Tale* the double image of the pure, lofty mother who goes through death and resurrection, and the pure, lovely daughter who reunites with the mother. In *Pericles* the daughter, Marina, has to endure the most awful trials; in *The Winter's Tale* the suffering of the soul lies in the destiny of the mother.

However, the most important thing is that the poet lets the Greek wisdom of the soul flow into Christian wisdom. In the New Age, the old mysteries have to be renewed. *The Winter's Tale* does not repeat the images of the Eleusinian drama, but metamorphoses these in a Christian sense. The power of individual love that ties Perdita to Florizel is Christian. This power leads here to redemption and resurrection. The "priestess" who is initiated in the secrets of the power of Christian love, *Paulina*, carries out, as a ritual act, the unveiling of the statue of Hermione, and calls it to life.

Perdita-Proserpina does not return out of the dark Hades underworld to the cosmic union of nature and the human soul, as in the Greek myth—and in the Greek myth she comes back only for a season, for Hades has given her the seeds of a pomegranate to eat, so that she cannot remain with her mother but has to return again and again to the realm of the dead. But the lost child returns from the light world of pastoral innocence to the "man who dwelt by a churchyard," the sinful, fallen man of the earth, chained to death. And this return is not of a temporary nature; it is for eternity.

For the initiated Greek, Persephone was the bearer of future salvation. The highest secret that was shown to the aspirants in Eleusis was the picture of the Virgin with the child Iacchus (Dionysus). This Iacchus god can be regarded as an expectation of Christ. Christ brings to humanity the power of the free "I" which for the Greek was still a future power that had to be born from the womb of the Persephone being.

In Perdita and Florizel this "I" power is working convincingly. Their love is the bond of two free, individual human beings, unfettered by their social difference, for they cannot know other than that Perdita is the daughter of the old shepherd. Their love does not shrink from the forces of heredity and social convention. The wrath of King Polyxenes cannot break the sovereign power of the "I." Perdita is the poetic image of the already Christianized soul. She has the Persephone being in herself as the past, but the future has already begun in her.

With the scene of Perdita giving flowers to people we are reminded of Ophelia. The unfortunate beloved of Prince Hamlet also gives out flowers, but she is insane. We see the most poignant, the most pitiable picture of the lost soul bride who perishes in the dark water of death and, by contrast, the royal shepherd's child, the shepherdly princess on the murmuring, blossoming sea-coast of Bohemia, filled to the brim with light, life and love! How can humanity ever sufficiently honor a poet who has bestowed on us such a mercy of transformation in images and words?

Time, Apollo, or a higher sun power?

Just as with *As You Like It*, in regard to *The Winter's Tale* we can pose the question whether Shakespeare does not owe the essence of his play to his model, in this case the story by Robert Greene. Most critics who consider this question point out that Shakespeare knows how to recreate the literary puppets of these models into living human beings, and that he adds a few figures to the story who particularly vivify the dramatic situations and add much color.

That is undoubtedly true, but we must not lose sight of the essential nature of certain of the changes he makes in the story, which suddenly lift it to a completely different level. In Greene's *Pandosto* the king whom Shakespeare calls Leontes turns inward through the judgment of the Apollo oracle. In Shakespeare, he rejects the judgment, as a result of which the power of Apollo receives a much more decisive character in the course of the play. At the news of Mamillius's death Leontes exclaims:

Apollo's angry; and the heavens themselves
Do strike at my injustice. [3.2]

When the queen then swoons, Leontes implores swift-punishing Apollo's pardon. Does the godhead answer this prayer? For the Greeks the gods could not be propitiated by repentance, only by sacrificial offerings. The judgment does not preclude the possibility of reconciliation: the lost child has to be found again. But what is the sacrifice Leontes has to make, what does he undertake to exculpate himself from the wrath of Apollo? Seemingly, he undertakes nothing. He makes no ritual sacrifices; he builds no sanctuary for the offended god; he even makes no effort to track down the lost child.

The process turns completely inward. He nourishes the consciousness of his guilt by a continued show of mourning; he dwells in his grief as it were. The one who supports him in this is not a Greek but a Christian "priestess," Paulina. Without giving it any emphasis, the poet lets the Greek element blend into the Christian element. A higher power, higher than Apollo, guides the further course of destiny toward the final reconciliation.

Greene calls his story the triumph of time. Time brings the truth to light. For Shakespeare this abstract concept of time becomes a most mysterious, living power which, through the working of Apollo, arranges the outer events to the good, while it directs through Paulina the inner process of death and resurrection.

The allegorical figure of Time with his long beard and his hourglass, who in awkward verses has to inform the public of what has been happening in sixteen years, appears awfully meager in Shakespeare's sublime approach to the mystery of destiny. A modern director could perhaps replace this unfortunate interpolation with music accompanied by a few wordless pictures.

In what ways does Shakespeare indicate the serving role of Apollo in the course of the drama? In a dream in which Hermione appears to him, Antigonus is guided to a place where the child may be preserved. The clown has gone hunting in the bad weather, with the result that two sheep became scared and ran away. The old shepherd looks for the sheep and finds the lost baby. A bear devours Antigonus. This surprising course of events betrays divine guidance. The dream with the character of an oracle belongs to the sphere of Apollo; the hunt and the bear indicate Artemis, Apollo's sister, who even more than Apollo is the protectress of mothers and newborn children.

At the shepherds' feast sixteen years later, Florizel appears as the representative of Apollo, the radiant, strong *kouros*. He says to Perdita, who is a little alarmed by their difference in social position, that the gods appeared on earth in the shape of lower figures because of their love for a mortal girl:

> Jupiter
> Became a bull, and bellow'd; the green Neptune
> A ram, and bleated; and fire-rob'd god,
> Golden Apollo, a poor humble swain,
> As I seem now. [4.4]

Apollo was honored as the shepherds' god, especially in Arcadia. But there is a big difference between these ancient gods and this Apollonian youth:

> Their transformations
> Were never for a piece of beauty rarer,
> Nor in a way so chaste, since my desires
> Run not before mine honour, nor my lusts
> Burn hotter than my faith. [4.4]

Florizel's morality is of a higher order than that of the Greek gods, who never controlled the burning of their lust. Among them, by the way, Apollo was one of the most austere.

In order to accentuate the contrast between the element of lust and Apollonian self-control, Shakespeare lets twelve shepherds perform a satyr dance to enliven the feast. All the figures around the loving couple are filled with egoistic motivations: the quarreling shepherdesses Mopsa and Dorcas, the silly clown, the rogue Autolycus, and Polyxenes who is concerned about his succession. Even the noble Camillo pursues his own interest of returning to Sicily. And the old shepherd trembles in fear for his life.

Only the purity of the two lovers shines out over all these human weaknesses. Their love is not egoistic; it is like a Christian sun gift. Florizel's falcon brought them together by flying over the property of the old shepherd.

The falcon is of old a sun symbol. Perdita calls the sun the light- and love-power that is unconcerned about differences between high and low within earthly confines, and therefore dissolves these differences:

> I was not much afeard; for once or twice
> I was about to speak, and tell him plainly
> The self-same sun that shines upon his court
> Hides not his visage from our cottage, but
> Looks on alike. [4.3]

She says this after Polyxenes furiously tried to break the love bond between his son and the charming shepherd's child with the hardest words and threats. But guided by the certainty of his love, Florizel makes his own decision:

> I am put to sea
> With her whom here I cannot hold on shore. [4.3]

He is not conscious of the circumstance that by leaving his country and renouncing his royal status and descent, he follows the intention of a higher disposition. The clever calculation of Camillo, who advises the inexperienced prince to travel to Sicily, with the intention to end up there himself when he betrays this to his king, may surprise us in such a noble person. But we see here none other than the guiding hand of the higher sun power, which does not shrink from using these means for the good of all.

Hope, faith and love

There is hardly another figure in all of Shakespeare's dramatic oeuvre that evokes our sympathy as strongly as Paulina. Her golden honesty, her courage and high spirit, her wisdom and unconditional faithfulness are so heartwarming that one never tires of listening to her. She is the one who holds the key to the drama. She guides both Leontes and Hermione through a process of mortification and catharsis that lasts for sixteen years. The poet leaves us guessing as to what this woman, herself so harshly tested by destiny, must have said and done to guide both her king and queen, so that the one penitent in his guilt, and the other suffering in innocence not only accept their bitter destiny, but are in the meantime prepared for the rebirth of their bond.

Her name indicates her inner secret. She is the only person in the play whose name reminds us immediately of the Christian impulse. In the final scene she stands and speaks as a priestess who fulfills a sacred, ritual act. Her house has become a temple where the ancient Apollo mystery finds fulfillment in the Christian mystery of the resurrection. The words that were inscribed on the inner frieze of the Apollo temple in Delphi— "Know Thyself"—receive their deepest significance in Paulina's house.

It is again no coincidence that in this scene Shakespeare uses three words, in different places in the text, which are commonly used to denote the Christian virtues: faith, hope, and love. These are also called the Pauline virtues, since the apostle first spoke of them in his letters.

Hermione, after her holy silence, is moved to speech by her kneeling child, and reveals that the hope the oracle had given for the preservation of the child, had kept her alive. It is evident that Paulina had always supported her in nourishing this hope, in developing it as a *virtue*.

Earlier, when the statue of Hermione is going to be called to life, Paulina says to all, but to Leontes in particular: "It is requir'ed you do awake your faith." *Faith*—there is no word that has been so misused and misunderstood among Christians as the word faith.

In the course of 2000 years of Christianity, to have faith, to believe, has come to mean that you accept something as true which you can neither prove nor understand. (The Church even says that you are not *allowed* to understand it.) Protestantism, especially Luther, ascribed this view of faith principally to St. Paul but, in so doing, interpreted the great apostle, faith, and Christianity in a one-sided manner. Luther, who had a thorough dislike of intellectual thinking, was not able to grasp that St. Paul understood by faith something entirely different from accepting through feeling something you don't understand through thinking. From the letters of St. Paul, however, we may conclude that faith in a Christian sense is not the passive acceptance of suprasensible facts which are then called "miracles," but a *virtue*, an activity therefore, which has to be trained.

Faith is a power in the soul that may be viewed as a Christian metamorphosis of what the Greeks called the virtue of wisdom. The wise Greek was able to translate suprasensible, divine truths into human thought forms. With this capacity one could understand the working of the divine in nature and in the human being.

However, the mystery of Christ's descent to earth, of his death and resurrection, cannot be understood in this way. This demands that wisdom itself be awakened to a higher level of understanding by the power of the resurrection itself. And that is faith.

St. Paul, who, after his experience near Damascus carried the resurrection as a living experience in himself, and who was guided throughout his entire further life by the power of the resurrection, exhorts human beings to develop the virtue of faith. But he knows that this virtue is but a blind fumbling without the virtue of love.

Unlike Hermione in her seclusion, for sixteen years Leontes did not nourish hope. He "dwelt by the churchyard" grieving for his wife and child. But the awareness of his guilt made him ripe for faith.

The miracle Paulina performs by calling the statue to life is no "unlawful business"; nor is it a theatrical display of self-importance, or a kind of solemn, dressed-up surprise. It is an inner act of initiation that is performed in the soul of Leontes, but in which the others participate:

Paulina:
It is requir'd
You do awake your faith. Then, all stand still;
Or those that think it is unlawful business
I am about, let them depart.
Leontes:
Proceed:
No foot shall stir.
Paulina:
Music, awake her: strike! (*Music.*)
'Tis time; descend; be stone no more; approach;
Strike all that look upon with marvel. Come;
I'll fill your grave up: stir; nay, come away;
Bequeath to death your numbness, for from him
Dear life redeems you.—You perceive she stirs:
(*Hermione comes down from the pedestal.*)
Start not; her actions shall be holy as
You hear my spell is lawful: do not shun her
Until you see her die again; for then
You kill her double. Nay, present your hand:
When she was young you woo'd her; now in age
Is she become the suitor! [5.3]

Even as human beings in their origin have come into being and have lived out of the divine love that was bestowed on them, so from a certain stage in their development they have to become bestowers of love themselves. Shakespeare's Pauline spirit knows this highest goal of humanity, and expresses its secret in a seemingly simple image and in the most simple words:

Nay, present your hand:
When she was young you woo'd her; now in age
Is she become the suitor!

And Leontes, taking Hermione's hand, says only: "O! She's warm." And he embraces her. The most common, everyday gesture, giving our fellow human being our hand, embracing the one for whom one feels affection, love, is here shown as a sacred archetypal image of love. No actor in the role of Leontes dare speak the words, "O! She's warm," without inner awareness of what is actually being enacted in this scene. He could run the risk of making people laugh instead of letting people share in a mystery.

The Pauline virtues, hope, faith, and love, born from the sacred sun-spring of Christ's resurrection, not only lead to the raising of the soul of death-fettered humanity, they form at the same time a threefold path of schooling leading to knowledge of the true essence of the human being. The temple inscription in Delphi, "Know Thyself," here finds its fulfillment.

How does Shakespeare show us this fulfillment in the final scene of his inexhaustibly rich *Tale*? Again, exclusively by dramatic means. By the power of Paulina's sacred magic, the gradual becoming human of Hermione is enacted before our eyes. First we see her physical appearance in the niche where she is standing as a statue. Time has engraved its traces in the full beauty of her body; her now older face expresses that the physical body is perishable. But before the majesty of the body, the mother temple of the divine nature, Perdita kneels down and reverently seeks to kiss its hand.

Then a second "miracle" reveals itself in the pretended stone counterfeit: it seems to breathe; the blood vessels seem to be filled with actual, flowing blood. Leontes is the first to perceive this; Polyxenes speaks it: "The very life seems warm upon her lip." In Leontes, the mortified penitent, the life in the statue similarly evokes the full power of the joy of life: he wants to kiss her. But Paulina holds him back so she can perform the third miracle: the ensoulment.

The body moves, it steps down from the niche and extends her hand to Leontes. Music sounds. For Shakespeare knows that human beings, as "immortal souls," bear the heavenly music of the stars in themselves (see *The Merchant of Venice*). When the soul has been awakened from death, it can again find its connection with another soul in love. However, only the fourth, the highest revelation of humanness brings complete fulfillment.

Camillo asks: "If she pertain to life, let her speak too." And Polyxenes: "Ay; and make 't manifest where she has lived, or how stol'n from the dead." Camillo asks about the capacity of speech; Polyxenes about her destiny. Speech is the expression of the "I" in the human being, the highest spiritual principle that works as a core in the ensouled, living body, and because of this, and with this, forms and undergoes a destiny on earth. For the awakening of the "I" Paulina needs the help of Perdita:

> Please you to interpose, fair madam: kneel,
> And pray your mother's blessing. Turn, good lady;
> Our Perdita is found. [5.3]

Perdita, the bearer of the kingly-shepherdly "I" force, the love bearer, was found. By her return, the divine severity and justice of destiny has grown into compassion and mercy. The "graces of the gods" may therefore descend on her, and all may share in this blessing.

7

THE TEMPEST

———

Justice and Love

Beyond death

The Tempest is rightly considered to be Shakespeare's final work. The drama about Henry VIII, although of a later date, is only partly by his hand. It is assumed that Fletcher wrote this play, possibly following a plan created by Shakespeare, who may also have written a few interesting scenes. No matter how beautiful these scenes may be, they are just an encore. The end, the farewell is *The Tempest*.

This play came into being shortly after *The Winter's Tale*, probably in the same year (1611). Five years later the poet died exactly on his 52nd birthday, April 23, 1616, the day of St. George, the patron saint of England.

When we, inspired by the deep reverence Goethe felt for Shakespeare (he called him a "being of a higher order") search for an answer to the riddle of the five last, "silent" years of the poet, we may be able to find it in the images of *The Tempest*. Here we need not look for the imaginative level behind the realistic and psychological aspects; the images of the play reveal their imaginative character immediately. They relate, above all else, to the catharsis of the soul. This motif, running like a golden thread through the entire oeuvre of the poet, is here presented in such a form that it reminds us more of a kind of purgatory than of a process that is enacted in earthly reality.

The isle of Prospero lies beyond death; it lies in the imaginative sphere of the elements and of the soul world. The terrors endured by Prospero's enemies are of the nature of soul torments suffered by malefactors after death. We can imagine that King Alonso, Sebastian, and Antonio have to begin a new life upon their return to Naples and Milan after they have sojourned on the island beyond death. But the same is true for Prospero. He has also gone through a process of change; he has concluded his life as a magician on the island.

Shakespeare must have felt his Tempest creation like a "full stop." Should he have had the desire to write additional dramas, he would have had to start from the beginning again. His wisdom held him back from this. After having formed the highest and most beautiful flower of his life's work, he followed the law of diastole and systole: after unfolding, contraction; after the revelation of the blossom, the secrecy of the seed.

Seed-forming is dying; dying is seed-forming. During the five years of "dying" during which the poet still lived as a distinguished citizen in his birthplace, Stratford-on-Avon, an event occurred in London that can be taken as a symbol: Shakespeare's theater, The Globe, burned to the ground during a performance of *King Henry VIII*. In addition to the famous theater itself, all the beautiful costumes, props and, probably, also precious manuscripts of the company were lost. This happened in 1613.

The first plays by Shakespeare that were preserved for posterity date back to 1592. In twenty-one years the entire dramatic oeuvre came into being, a world-all, a globe of poetry, more real than earthly reality. This world of higher reality had its dwelling place in the theater named The Globe. When the creative genius who filled this Globe with his images went into retirement, the outer dwelling place went up in flames.

Or did the loss of his beloved theater undermine the life forces of the poet? We do not know. But the most perfect, the most beautiful stage play ever written by a human being, *The Tempest*, lies in front of us as a farewell; a farewell that took place even before the fire at The Globe:

> Our revels are now ended: these our actors,
> As I foretold you, were all spirits and
> Are melted into air, into thin air;
> And like the baseless fabric of this vision
> The cloud-capp'd towers, the gorgeous palaces,
> The solemn temples, the great globe itself,
> Yea, all which it inherit, shall dissolve,
> And like this insubstantial pageant faded,
> Leave not a rack behind: We are such stuff
> As dreams are made of, and our little life
> Is rounded with a sleep. [4.1]

These words, spoken by Prospero to his son-in-law, Prince Ferdinand, have to be the most unusual engagement speech anyone can imagine. For they are not spoken out of a normal consciousness, but from a consciousness beyond death. The sleep by which "our little life is rounded" is not a state of not-being. This "nothing" from which all that is originates, and to which it again returns, is the highest reality that human beings find only when they have found themselves.

The old councilor Gonzalo has discovered some of this secret. When the enchantment of the three malefactors has been broken and the happy couple has been shown to their restored eyes, he exclaims (5. 1):

> ... in one voyage
> Did Claribel her husband find at Tunis;

> And Ferdinand, her brother, found a wife
> Where he himself was lost; Prospero his dukedom
> In a poor isle; and all of ourselves,
> When no man was his own. [5.1]

In ordinary earthly life we are not "our own." We live in a dream of a perishable reality. Above it, or behind it, stands our true self. This true self is not perishable; it comes from the "sleep that rounds our little life." The "sleep" is the higher realm of spiritual reality. To find oneself there is the great theme of becoming human.

Two portals lead to the possibility of finding our true self: the portal of death and the portal of initiation. Both portals, which are in truth one and the same, open exclusively for the purified soul that has vanquished all that is transitory, to which egoism and baseness keep it fettered. Prospero's isle, the place beyond death, is the mystery center where this catharsis is achieved.

The story

Act I

Prospero, Duke of Milan, has given most of the government of his state into the hands of his brother Antonio, so that he can dedicate himself wholly to his occult studies. This has awakened a devil in Antonio. Prospero's confidence calls forth evil in him. He arrogates more and more power to himself and, in order to consolidate his position, he becomes a vassal of the King of Naples and complies with the latter's demands of a very high tribute and the destruction of Prospero and his descendants.

Prospero and his three-year-old daughter Miranda are suddenly dragged from their castle and set down on a wreck off the coast where they are left at the mercy of wind and waves. A noble Neapolitan with the name of Gonzalo takes care that also some food, water, and

Prospero's most important books, ceremonial vestments, and instruments are put on the wreck.

By divine providence father and daughter land on an island, where Prospero dedicates himself to the education of Miranda, and where his magical power enables him to gain control over the aerial spirit Ariel and the monster Caliban, who both have to serve him, each in his own way.

When the play begins, twelve years have passed since Prospero's landing on the island. By coincidence, his enemies are in a fleet in the vicinity of the island. Prospero knows this and has computed that the configuration of his stars is favorable to him for a reckoning, if he now uses the powers at his disposal to this purpose.

He has told Ariel to beguile the fleet with a storm scene, in which the ship of the Neapolitan king seemingly founders. The royal passengers, including King Alonso himself, his son Ferdinand, his brother Sebastian, and also Prospero's brother Antonio, along with the venerable Gonzalo, have to be put on land in the most remote part of the island. Prince Ferdinand has to be separated from his traveling companions and end up alone somewhere else.

Ariel has executed his commission to the letter: no one is injured; no one's clothes have been spoiled by salt water; the scattered ships have gathered together again and, with the flags at half-mast because of the supposed death of the king, they are on their way back to Naples. The royal ship is anchored, trim and neat, in a hidden creek, the crew asleep. Prince Ferdinand is sitting by himself, sad and lonely, somewhere on the island.

Prospero is content with his aerial spirit, but when the latter implores him to finally give him his promised freedom, he becomes angry. He reminds Ariel that he had freed him from the horrible witch Sycorax, who had held the poor thing caught in a split tree trunk because it had rejected her disgusting advances. This is how Prospero had found the poor aerial spirit who had been sitting there whining for twelve years. In the meantime Sycorax died, leaving behind on the island only the monstrous fruit of her womb, Caliban.

Prospero liberated Ariel by his magical power and also subjected Caliban who then had to serve him like a slave. Having become more docile again by this reminder and by the threat of fresh torture, Ariel receives a new order. In the shape of a mermaid, he has to entice Ferdinand to Prospero's cell with miraculous singing.

Caliban has to gather firewood. He also protests against his servitude, but in a malevolent manner: he curses his master. Prospero becomes even angrier at this slave and remonstrates with him that all the good he has done for him is now for nought. He has lovingly cared for him, has taught him speech and civility, but has had to keep him down with violence and punishment as an incorrigible piece of malevolence since Caliban had tried to rape Miranda. The monster regrets that he had failed in that; otherwise he would have peopled the island with Calibans. Sulking he goes to find firewood, bowing to Prospero's power.

Prince Ferdinand is led to Prospero and Miranda by Ariel's singing. It is Prospero's intention to unite these two young people in a bond of love. He succeeds: they fall head over heels in love with each other. Prospero, however, finds it advisable to slow them down a little, and treats Ferdinand very sternly.

Miranda is upset at the hardness of her father as he pushes his darling away when she stands up for Ferdinand. The young prince also has to bow to the power of the magician, and is forced to perform arduous and lowly work.

Act II

Elsewhere on the island, King Alonso is deeply dejected; he fears that his son Ferdinand was drowned. Gonzalo tries to comfort him, but is ridiculed by Antonio and Sebastian. To distract his king, the old councilor expounds how he would form a utopian state if he were king of the island.

Alonso, Gonzalo, and two noblemen of the king's entourage fall asleep. Antonio and Sebastian remain awake and begin to plot a wicked plan: they will kill Alonso and Gonzalo so that Sebastian can become king of Naples. When they have already drawn their swords to commit the murders, Ariel becomes aware of the danger and wakes everyone up. The two villains act as if they had to defend the sleeping king from wild animals. They continue their trek through the island.

Carrying his bundle of firewood, Caliban runs into two other shipwrecked men, the steward Stefano, who had floated ashore on a cask of Malaga wine and has had a good go at it, and Trinculo, the jester. At first, the monster is mortally afraid of these figures because he thinks that they are evil spirits sent by Prospero to punish him. But when Stefano lets him taste some wine from a jar he has filled from the cask, the monster becomes merry. He worships Stefano like a god and promises to show him the wonders of the island. He performs a drunken dance and roars: "Freedom, high-day! Freedom!"

Act III

Prince Ferdinand performs day-laborer's work, but he does not mind the toil because of his proximity to Miranda who shows great compassion for him. In a conversation with his "mistress" Ferdinand confesses his love. Miranda responds in the most heart-warming manner. Prospero, unnoticed by the loving couple, hears them and is struck by the purity of their feelings.

Stefano, Trinculo, and Caliban, all of them now well-oiled, are spied upon by Ariel. The monster now recognizes Stefano as his master, but is not on good terms with the jester; he proposes to go and kill Prospero. Invisible to the threesome, Ariel calls out now and then: "Thou liest!" which is ascribed to Trinculo, who then gets a beating from Stefano.

When Caliban starts to dance around for joy because Stefano has promised to murder the sorcerer and take possession of his pretty daughter, they hear music played by the invisible Ariel. The two men, upset at first by the ghostly tune, are set at ease by Caliban, and they embark on their undertaking, led on by Ariel's music.

The totally exhausted company of King Alonso is now brought to Prospero's place, and from a high point he leads and oversees the course of events. Spirits bring a table set with delicious food. When Alonso, Antonio, and Sebastian sit down to eat, Ariel appears in the form of a harpy. With lashing words he denounces their crime against Prospero. They will now experience the revenge of destiny. The sea and the storm have thrown them onto the island, where they will die a slow and miserable death. Ferdinand has already been torn away from them. Their demise is certain; nothing will help short of repentance and a chastised heart. There is a thunder clap and the harpy is gone. With mockery in their faces the spirits clear the table.

Prospero is very happy with the game of Ariel and his helpers. His enemies are now in his power; their souls are in total turmoil and their minds are bewildered. He hastens to Ferdinand and Miranda.

Alonso, deeply disturbed by an awareness of guilt, wants to go and look for his son in the bottomless sea and join him in the mud. Sebastian and Antonio, randomly fighting invisible powers, follow him. Gonzalo exhorts the noblemen to follow the bewildered sinners and to keep them from desperate actions.

Act IV

Prospero bestows his daughter Miranda on Ferdinand. The latter has brilliantly overcome the trials imposed on him to test his love. But Prospero warns him with great emphasis not to "break her virgin knot" before the sacred marriage ceremony has taken place, because otherwise no heavenly blessing can rest on their union.

He orders Ariel to summon his host of spirits so that with his magical powers Prospero can show the young couple an exquisite work of art. After once more urging his son-in-law to control himself, Prospero calls up an impressive Greek masked play for his children.

Iris, the messenger of the gods, invites Ceres and Juno to bestow their blessing on Ferdinand and Miranda. Provocative Venus with her whimsical little son has disappeared because she saw that the power of her temptations was not equal to the couple's true love. After the blessing by the two goddesses follows a graceful dance of nymphs and reapers.

Suddenly Prospero breaks off the performance. He had forgotten the plot of the monster and his cronies against his life. Miranda and Ferdinand are most upset because of Prospero's sudden anger. But the latter speaks to them in heartening words and reveals to Ferdinand the secret of the fleeting appearance of "our little life rounded with a sleep."

Ariel reports that he has led the drunken threesome through thorn bushes to the cesspool with the magic of his music. They are tramping around up to their neck in the stinking stuff. Ariel must now hang ceremonial vestments from Prospero's cell on a clothes line as bait to lure thieves. On tiptoe, the wet, stinking threesome approach Prospero's cell. Stefano and Trinculo are unhappy with Caliban because he had told them that the little sprite that had led them to the cesspool was innocent. The beautiful vestments are discovered and, in spite of Caliban's warnings, the two knaves can't keep themselves from stealing them. Prospero and Ariel then set their servant spirits on them in the shape of hunting dogs. Yelling loudly they take to their heels, forced on and tormented by the host of spirits.

Act V

Prospero's great work is nearing completion. Alonso, Antonio, and Sebastian, still overcome by their frenzy, and faithfully guarded by their fellow travelers, have been led by Ariel very near to Prospero's dwelling place. The virtuous spirit is full of compassion for the sinners whose plight has reduced their royal bearing to jelly. Prospero is touched by this feeling of sympathy, and his higher insight opts against his thirst for revenge. He wants to forgive. Ariel has to break their enchantment and bring them to Prospero.

Prospero evokes the spirits of the elements with whose help he has conjured up the tempest and performed his magic. He abjures his magic and implores for heavenly music that can cure the injured spiritual capacities of the three guilty ones. When this happens he wants to break his magic wand and throw his book into the sea.

Alonso and his entourage are now led into a magical circle. Prospero addresses them while solemn music sounds. Once again they are confronted with their crimes. Prospero then lets Ariel adorn him with his ducal ceremonial vestments, and orders his servant to awake the captain and boatswain of the royal ship from their sleep and bring them to his cell. Alonso, Sebastian, and Antonio recover the presence of their minds, and recognize Prospero who forgives them all for their crimes; but they remain baffled by the whole situation.

Alonso then speaks of the loss of his beloved son, and Prospero reports that he has also lost a child. At the surprised question of the king he invites them to look inside his cell. The cell opens, and Ferdinand and Miranda become visible. The reunion of father and son, the rapture of Miranda when she sees so many handsome people, the emotion of the good Gonzalo and the joy of Alonso at the union of his son with the beautiful girl—all of this is like a golden sun breaking through the clouds after the terror of an awful storm.

The captain and the boatswain come with the report that the ship is safe and sound and is ready to put to sea. They say that they feel as if they were brought here by a magical power. Ariel has seen to everything,

At this point Caliban and his unsavory cronies are brought in with their stolen vestments; they are black and blue from the blows of the spirits. Their drunken courage has pretty well evaporated. Caliban wants to be wiser from now on and no longer take a drunkard for a god and a fool for his prophet. Prospero chases them inside to return the stolen clothes, but for the rest they are mercifully treated.

The company is invited to spend the night in Prospero's cell and put to sea for Naples the next morning, where the marriage of Ferdinand and Miranda will be celebrated. Prospero will then return to Milan. Ariel receives his freedom. Prospero speaks the epilogue:

> Now my charms are all o'erthrown,
> And what strength I have's mine own,
> Which is most faint: now, 'tis true,
> I must be here confined by you,
> Or sent to Naples. Let me not,
> Since I have my dukedom got,
> And pardon'd the deceiver, dwell
> In this bare island by your spell;

But release me from my bands
With the help of your good hands.
Gentle breath of yours my sails
Must fill, or else my project fails,
Which was to please. Now I want
Spirits to enforce, art to enchant;
And my ending is despair
Unless I be relieved by prayer;
Which pierces so, that it assaults
Mercy itself, and frees all faults.
As you from crimes would pardon'd be,
Let your indulgence set me free. [5.1]

The island of the soul

In the previous studies, particularly in that of *The Winter's Tale*, it was pointed out that in Shakespeare's last works important themes from his earlier plays return in metamorphosed form. These metamorphoses relate to the inner changes undergone by the poet himself. After the dark inferno world of the great tragedies, where the demise of the soul is shown, we now see the dawning glory of a new light realm. The motif of the catharsis of the soul, so clearly present already in *The Merchant of Venice* and *A Midsummer Night's Dream*, comes to the fore ever more impressively, and culminates in *The Winter's Tale* and *The Tempest*.

In *The Winter's Tale* we experience the raising of the soul; in *The Tempest*, the rebirth of the soul. I am making a distinction between these two concepts, which are most intimately related, in order to indicate that in *The Tempest* the poet penetrates even more deeply into the mystery of the human soul than in his *Tale*. But that is not the only difference.

The Tempest contains aspects of the Hamlet situation: fratricide and its retribution (therefore the theme of justice), but also motifs from the tragedy of *King Lear*: the ruler who entrusts his realm into the hands of another and, in so doing, involuntarily intensifies malevolence in those in whom he has the most confidence. There is also the father-daughter relationship, and let us not overlook the storm. If in Perdita we can see sorrowful Ophelia reborn, we may view Miranda as a new Cordelia. The mighty storm of perdition in *King Lear*, which reflects the madness of the tragic old man and the ruin of his soul, is metamorphosed into the purifying magical storm of the wise Prospero.

Moreover, *The Tempest* is the perfect drama of nature forces and music. The more earth-bound nature spirits of *A Midsummer Night's Dream*—Oberon, Titania, Puck—are here metamorphosed into the lovely and tender, but much more powerful, nature spirit Ariel, who has no relationship with the dreamy moon sphere, but with the lucid and lofty Jupiter sphere.

While in *The Merchant of Venice* the most profound words are spoken about music, the isle of Prospero is all music. Everything that happens there happens by music. The storm itself, with which the play opens, is music. Alonso has heard it:

> The winds did sing it to me; and the thunder,
> That deep and dreadful organ pipe, pronounced
> The name of Prosper... [3.3]

Let us not forget that a great admirer of Shakespeare, Ludwig van Beethoven, was inspired by *The Tempest* to compose his grandiose piano sonatas, the *Apassionata* and the *Storm Sonata*. With the "masked play" Shakespeare weaves the Greek mystery element, that always lives in him, into the imaginations of the island world.

And finally, we see the metamorphosis and culmination of evil. Facing the classical evildoers, the ambitious, the violent, the unscrupulous, the traitors and mockers such as Antonio and Sebastian, men of the caliber of Don John (*Much Ado about Nothing*), Iago (*Othello*), or Edgar, the bastard in *King Lear*, here stands the witch's cub, this piece of concentrated, monstrous evil, Caliban. Shylock too is unmatched in his evil, but he is still a human being; he still possesses greatness in his sinister thirst for revenge. Caliban is a direct imagination of the dark forces in the human soul; he is pure baseness.

And yet, just like Shylock, Caliban also stirs us to compassion. Shylock justifies his thirst for revenge with his hatred of the Christian Antonio who despises and tramples on him, a Jew. When in the end he is condemned to hand over all his possessions and, on top of that, adopt the religion of his enemies, we experience that as inhuman. However, there is profound wisdom in this sentence. Shylock can only be redeemed by Christ. What is imposed on him from outside is what he should inwardly attain in freedom. But the curtain closes on this soul drama at the end of the fourth act. Shylock leaves a broken man, no word of repentance crosses his lips. We follow his shuffling steps and bent back with intense compassion, and with the anxious question: Will this soul be forever stuck in its obduracy?

Caliban justifies his hatred of Prospero because the latter has violated his property rights on the island. If he had been successful in raping Miranda he would have peopled the whole island with monsters like himself. This was prevented, but as a result, he ended up in deeper slavery and torment. Evil itself knows no happiness. Sometimes Caliban weeps, when the wondrous sounds of the island awaken softer feelings in him:

> Be not afeard; the isle is full of noises,
> Sounds and sweet airs that give delight and hurt not.
> Sometimes a thousand twangling instruments
> Will hum about mine ears; and sometime voices,

> That, if I then had wak'd after long sleep,
> Will make me sleep again; and then in dreaming
> The clouds, methought, would open and show riches
> Ready to drop upon me: that, when I wak'd,
> I cried to dream again. [3.2]

When on the day following the storm the ship will take all human beings from the isle, Ariel and Caliban remain behind. Ariel has been liberated; is Caliban also free? Is evil redeemed, or merely repulsed?

In fairy tales, the frog, the bear, or the monster changes into a handsome prince. Here that is not the case. Why in the fairy tales and not here? Because the frog, the bear, and the monster do not desire the princess, but love her. Caliban and Ferdinand have to be viewed together. Ferdinand is for a short time put in the same kind of slavery as Caliban. But he performs this work as a love service for Miranda. Caliban knows no love, only lust. Not by coincidence does Prospero warn Ferdinand twice to keep his lust under control.

We can view the various figures in the play as components of Prospero's soul, and the island as a world in which all the events of the day of the storm depict processes in this soul. We will then discover that the triumph of Ferdinand's and Miranda's chaste love opens a portal to introspection and catharsis in Prospero's being. He not only overcomes the base element in himself (Caliban), he redeems it, at least in part. Caliban remains behind, no less a monster than he was before, but a slightly wiser monster.

All people bear the total of their guilt, all their egotism, as a lower double in the depths of their being. In one human life we are not able to redeem this evil double completely, even if we honestly strive for moral perfection. But we can redeem a part of this demonic being in ourselves. What is left in us of this shadow and selfish monstrosity when we die, has to wait until we take this dark companion up again in the next life on earth so that we can then make another step in its redemption through selfless love.

We know how marvelously Shakespeare revealed evil in his dramas; but in *The Tempest*, he penetrated this mystery more profoundly than in any other play. The island itself is the most prodigious metamorphosis of the "other place" of which I wrote in the study of *As You Like It*. More than the Athenian wood or the Forest of Arden, more than the coast of Bohemia or the realm of Belmont, the isle of Prospero is a mystery place with its trials, transformative experiences, catharsis, and wisdom revelations. It is the island of the soul, a utopia that is not situated in the world but in the innermost depths of the soul. It is the battleground of white and black magic which, contending with each other for the upper hand, are both vanquished by a higher principle: love.

The soul of the island, the essence of the soul world, is Miranda. Her name is a Latin word that means "she who is to be admired." To protect her is Prospero's aim; to possess her is Caliban's aim, and when he lacks the power to achieve this he urges his drunken "god" Stefano on to this desire.

Only by the power of his white magic is Prospero able to protect his daughter and thus preserve her. The moment he bestows her on Ferdinand, who at his first encounter with her had recognized her as the miracle, the goddess of the island, he is able to make the highest step in his development. The love that transcends all magic broadens in Prospero's soul to include compassion for his enemies. This opens true freedom in him. He becomes able to let go of his magical power; he can now stand before us as a human being in his own weak strength. In his epilogue he asks us to confirm his achievement of humanness by showing him our approval. Otherwise he has to remain on his island.

In truth, it is not by his hard sorcery that the Caliban-force is subdued in Prospero, but by love. Only by giving away his highest possession does Prospero obtain it, for when Miranda finds her prince, Prospero finds himself, just as they all find themselves on the island.

What is Miranda, the pure essence of the soul world, looking for? She searches for the spirit. And she recognizes it immediately when she first sees Ferdinand:

> *Prospero:*
> The fringed curtains of thine eye advance,
> And say what thou seest yond.
> *Miranda:*
> What is't? a spirit?
> Lord, how it looks about! Believe me, sir,
> It carries a brave form. But 'tis a spirit. [1.2]

Isn't it delightful to hear how Shakespeare takes both "moments of recognition," relativises their loftiness and holiness with his very light and mild humor, and thus sets them down on the earth? Listen to Ferdinand when he sees Miranda:

> Most sure the goddess
> On whom these airs attend! Vouchsafe, my prayer
> May know, if you remain upon this island;
> And that you will some good instruction give,
> How I may bear me here: My prime request,
> Which I do last pronounce, is, O you wonder!
> If you be maid or no?

And Miranda very simply replies:

> No wonder, sir;
> But certainly a maid.

Prospero's answer to Miranda, when she says with great conviction that "'tis a spirit," is as follows:

> No, wench; it eats and sleeps and has such senses

As we have, such: This gallant, which thou seest
Was in the wreck: and but he's something stain'd
With grief, that's beauty's canker, thou might'st call him
A goodly person: he has lost his fellows,
And strays about to find them. [1.2]

In the following sections I will go deeper into some of the motifs only briefly indicated here.

White and black magic

Caliban is Sycorax's cub, a blue-eyed witch who was exiled from Algiers because of her black magical abominations. Because of one deed she was kept alive, but pregnant or no she was put on land by sailors. There she brought up her misshapen son and Ariel entered into her service. Because Ariel could not and would not respond to her earthly passions, she had more powerful servants put him into a split pine tree that pinched him so tightly that he could not escape. She died and left the island to Caliban who, like a nature being led by instinct and passion, acted as a dumb and animal-like king over the island, until Prospero arrived with his little daughter.

The witch Sycorax is the counter-image to Prospero. Their destinies show similarities, but in a polar sense. Prospero is expelled from Milan, not for his malevolence but for his goodness. He had acquired occult knowledge and magical capacities, but he exercised these in ascetic loneliness. He also did not use this power for himself, not even to defend himself, for he let himself be overcome by his enemies.

He made only one mistake, just as Sycorax had done only one good thing: he withdrew from his responsibility as reigning duke. His life too is spared; he too arrives on the island with a child. However, he is not brought there by human beings but by divine providence.

He frees Ariel from the pinching pine tree, takes him

into his service, and immerses himself in his studies by which he becomes a master of magic. He brings up his daughter Miranda and forms her into a human being in whom an innate naturalness and gentleness are combined with nobility and a living knowledge of heavenly and earthly things.

He also tries to ennoble the monster Caliban by teaching him language and culture with endless patience. He fails in this intended metamorphosis of evil. Caliban wants to assault Miranda.

The black-magical impulse represented by Sycorax is governed by Satan/Ahriman. In *The Tempest* this spirit is called Setebos, a Patagonian god whose name Shakespeare must have found in a travel report. It is Satan's intention to animalize humanity. Prospero is able to prevent the growth of such a bestial human race on the island, but he only succeeds in this by subduing the monster by force.

We have already seen that this can be viewed as an as-yet-unsolved problem within Prospero's own being. He pushes Caliban more deeply into evil by his good magic, just as he did with Antonio by his faithful trust and confidence.

The union of the pure soul being of Miranda with the hot monster is thus prevented, just as in the past another unholy connection did not take place on the island: the sinister history of Sycorax and Ariel is indicated by the poet with extreme reluctance:

> And, for thou wast a spirit too delicate
> To act her earthy and abhorr'd commands,
> Refusing her grand 'hests ... [1.2]

We can surmise that this means that Sycorax had wanted to force Ariel into sexual intercourse with her. If this suspicion is correct, we find there the exact counter-image of the saga of Merlin, the great Celtic magician.

For this saga relates how a pure nun is impregnated by a luciferic spirit that is called an air demon. The being thus conceived, Merlin, becomes the great magician of the West, the educator of King Arthur.

If a union between the good air spirit Ariel and the impure witch had taken place, it could perhaps have produced a magician with the same power as Merlin, but of a malicious nature. Satan needs such magicians in order to push humanity into perdition and into an animalistic state. In lieu of the all-powerful, impure magician who, if he had been born, would have turned the island into the center of his black-magical conquest of the world, just as Klingsor projected his destructive forces from Sicily into Europe, the pure magician Prospero arrives on the island, as a result of which the process of becoming human can be guided to a good end.

This line of thought may appear overly speculative. However, it is my conviction that in *The Tempest* Shakespeare touches on the incredibly profound apocalyptic problem of the "white" and "black" spiritual powers in the guidance of humanity. Modern human beings habitually tend to hear things about magic, both good and evil, with a good deal of skepticism. Materialism has deprived us of any and all possibility to understand the phenomenon of magic, and therefore we deny its existence. Magic is the utilization of spiritual powers to intervene directly into the physical order of things and beings, for the purpose of effecting change.

Natural magic, which is still practiced in some indigenous cultures, is grounded in the ability of a person who is schooled in this to exercise an influence on beings that "inhabit" seemingly soulless objects, by controlling (will) forces that usually remain completely subconscious. There are also higher forms of magic, the influence of which reaches into the astral (psychic) sphere.

Shakespeare knew and recognized the reality of magic. In his day there were still people who practiced magic, just as there continue to be such people even today, but in modern times the practice of magic tends to the dark side, or is entirely dark (think of *Faust*). The age of magic is past.

In the far distant past, the greatest battle ever fought on earth occurred between tribes that were led by black magicians (shamans) and a people that was guided by white magicians. In Persian sagas we find an echo of this battle in the stories of the great Iranian hero Rustam. The Turanian nomads of central Asia fought against the good magic of the Iranian people which was led by the great spiritual leader and arch-magician Zarathustra around 6000 BCE.

At stake in this battle was the human being. Good magic was directed toward ennobling the earth, its flora and fauna. It was obtained by initiation in the mystery of the Most High God, the Sun Spirit or Logos, whom the Iranians called Ahura Mazdao. Dark magic fettered the human being to the earth. It was obtained by systematic murder and incest in the mysteries of Ahriman/Satan. During the eras of the old Asian cultures, in Egypt, and far into Greek and Hellenistic times there were magicians of both the good and the evil kind. That was also the case in the Celtic West, in America, and in Africa.

The stories of the good magicians tell primarily of miraculous healings and raisings from the dead. These individuals were initiates who, not only by their knowledge but also by their highly developed will forces, had access to the divine-spiritual world. They were justifiably revered as gods; examples include Orpheus, Asclepius, the Sicilian wizard Empedocles, and the later Apollonius of Tyana, world-famous contemporary of Jesus.

Some people would like to view the "miracles"

performed by Jesus also as magic. However, this is a serious misjudgment of Christianity. Jesus emphatically rejected magic during the temptations in the wilderness. The miracles related by the gospels *in no instance intervene in the freedom of human beings*, which all magical deeds, including those for the good, invariably do. Jesus performed no magical miracles, but through him was working the Christ, the Sun Logos, who pervades the world of earth with the working of the divine spirit that leads human beings to their own free spirit being, so that they, with their own "weak strength," can yet share in higher worlds.

So long as humanity was not yet mature enough to develop its own free "I," it had to be guided by magicians. With the coming of Christ the era of magic came to an end. We see therefore that all great Christian initiates relinquish their magical capacities.

Let us certainly not presume that the magical works mentioned by Prospero in his famous invocation of the nature spirits are mere poetical fantasies of Shakespeare:

> Ye elves of hills, brooks, standing lakes, and groves;
> And ye that on the sands with printless foot
> Do chase the ebbing Neptune, and do fly him
> When he comes back; you demiputtets that
> By moonshine do the green sour ringlets make,
> Whereof the ewe not bites; and you whose pastime
> Is to make midnight mushrooms, that rejoice
> To hear the solemn curfew; by whose aid,
> Weak masters though ye be, I have bedimm'd
> The noontide sun, call'd forth the mutinous winds,
> And 'twixt the green sea and the azured vault
> Set roaring war: to the dread rattling thunder
> Have I given fire, and rifted Jove's stout oak
> With his own bolt; the strong-based promontory
> Have I made shake; and by the spurs pluck'd up

The pine and cedar; graves, at my command,
Have waked their sleepers, oped and let them forth
By my so potent art. But this rough magic
I here abjure. [5.1]

The high initiates of the white path are indeed capable of such deeds, but they do not use these capacities because, in imitation of Christ, they wish to respect the freedom of the human being in the most absolute sense.

Prospero's astrological wisdom enabled him to read in the starry constellations that he could seize his opportunity of revenge of the injustice that was done to him. The Jupiter moment that returns in a rhythm of twelve years (the time of one revolution of the planet around the sun) creates a new possibility of a turn in destiny. Twelve years earlier, Prospero arrived on the island and freed Ariel. Twelve years before that, Sycorax's diabolical intentions had been thwarted by Ariel's refusal to do her bidding. Prospero, who has increased his occult powers to the highest level, can now penalize his enemies like a god of revenge. He can turn the island into a world of hell from which there is no return.

A mighty divine wrath rises in him like a hurricane, and he transforms his inner world into a magically invoked tempest, into the roaring sea, the fierce lightning bolts, and raging thunder. But he is not only the father of revenge, he is also Miranda's father. It is his will that out of this judgment, out of the triumph of justice, life's happiness will be born for his beloved child. He wants to unite her with Prince Ferdinand.

He can read in the stars that the destiny moment for this too has arrived, but the love that has to unite these two souls is not something he can create by magic. This has to arise in them in freedom. All Prospero can do is watch if this miracle will be enacted. But if it succeeds, he can purify and test the bonding process by apparent resistance; although even here he has to wait and see whether the character of the young prince has sufficient strength. He has to wait and see whether the young man, whom he subjects to Caliban-like slavery, will not be seized by Caliban-like desire.

When love and purity triumph here, Prospero uses his magical powers to show the two lovers the sublime masked play of the spirits. Ferdinand exclaims:

> Let me live here ever;
> So rare a wonder'd father, and a wise,
> Makes this place paradise. [4.1]

Here Paradise, there the hell of damnation? In between, a new cluster of evil has formed around Caliban. Prospero had forgotten about it, and when he remembers the evil plot against his life again he flies into a rage.

Why is he so furious? Not because he is afraid of the drunken murderers, but because this makes him conscious of the fact that there is an unredeemed demon living in himself. Between the triumph of justice and the triumph of chaste love a devil can still wiggle its way in; it can be overcome, but it will resume its attack time and time again:

> Sir, I am vex'd;
> Bear with my weakness; my old brain is troubled,
> Be not disturb'd with my infirmity. [4.1]

Then again at the beginning of Act 5, Shakespeare reveals the deeper meaning of his drama. When *mercy* awakens in Prospero, evoked in him by the unforgettable Ariel; when he is ready to forgive in lieu of retaliation then he realizes that his sorcery has to yield; his sorcery that from "white magic" had already developed into "rough magic," the first step on the way to "black magic." He recognizes that his magic has bound the nature spirits to his will instead of releasing them from their earthbound state. Now he can fulfill his promise to Ariel, for he has himself achieved the freedom of his "nobler reason."

The process of catharsis in him has come to completion. He ends not as a god but as a human being. His magic is transformed into prayer. He prays for heavenly music to heal the guilty souls, and, at the end, he prays for mercy on himself:

> And my ending is despair
> Unless I be relieved by prayer;
> Which pierces so, that it assaults
> Mercy itself, and frees all faults. [Epilogue]

Shakespeare's "Utopia"

Gonzalo, who is highly esteemed by Prospero because he is honorable and had shown love and concern at the time of Prospero's exile, is a humorless, well-meaning chatterbox, a councilor of the type of Polonius but more likeable. It was a great idea for Shakespeare to sketch this noble figure in King Alonso's retinue as someone whom Englishmen call a bore. Only a person with such a good, but colorless character can survive in the company of villains. And yet this tiresome moral talker has a frame of mind that always enables him to sense a situation just right. For instance, he is the only one in the group who is struck by the fact that their clothes had remained bright and fresh after they had been drenched in the sea. He has a feeling for the miraculous nature of the island, just as Ferdinand in his own way also has.

Influenced by this feeling, Gonzalo develops the picture of a utopian society that he would found if he were the ruler of the island:

Gonzalo:
I' th' commonwealth I would by contraries

Execute all things; for no kind of traffic
Would I admit; no name of magistrate;
Letters should not be known; no use of service,
of riches, poverty; no contracts,
Successions; bound of land, tilth, vineyard, none;
No use of metal, corn, or wine, or oil;
No occupation; all men idle, all;
And women too; but innocent and pure;
No sovereignty.
Sebastian:
Yet he would be king on't.
Antonio:
The latter end of his commonwealth forgets the be-
ginning.
Gonzalo:
All things in common nature should produce,
Without sweat or endeavor; treason, felony,
Sword, pike, knife, gun, or need of any engine,
Would I not have; but Nature should bring forth
Of its own kind, all foison, all abundance,
To feed my innocent people.
Sebastian:
No marrying 'mong his subjects?
Antonio:
None, man; all idle: whores and knaves.
Gonzalo:
I would with such perfection govern, sir,
To excel the Golden Age. [2.1]

Without troubling himself about the ill-natured mockery of his companions or the despairing aversion of his king, Gonzalo sketches a paradisal state. Why does Shakespeare insert this superfluous silly talk into this otherwise so very compact play?

When we let go of the widespread view that *The Tempest* is a romantic fantasy play with at best an allegorical meaning, and when we learn to see this play more and more as a mystery drama, the nonsensical pratter of Gonzalo puts us on an extremely interesting track.

Since Plato described the model of an ideal state in his *Republic*, a whole series of such perfect societies have been designed on paper, following his example. They are called *utopias,* after Thomas More's famous book of that title (1517). The utopian idea plays a very big role in the history of humanity, because all forms of society are derived from the archetypal longing of human beings for a state of happiness and harmony. In historic cultures, there remained a dim memory of such a condition deemed to have existed in a far distant past. It was spoken of as a "Golden Age," and understood as a state of guiltless purity and peaceful life together.

It is, however, very significant that this paradisal state seems to exclude the principle of freedom, and that the establishment of such a society in later times is only possible under the strong authority of the state. The mockers Antonio and Sebastian put their fingers on the sore spot in Gonzalo's discourse: "Yet he would be king on't."

In most utopias private property is abolished because it is considered to be the basic cause of all disharmony. The land, or the produce of the land, is equally divided among all, as it was, for instance, in the military state of Sparta in ancient Greece. There is no doubt, of course, that greed, personal thirst for power and excessive wealth lead to oppression and social injustice which, in turn, provoke crime and rebellion. But the abolition of private property does not abolish egotistic tendencies in the human being. We see, therefore, that in utopian states these are forcefully suppressed and punished. In this connection, Thomas More's solution is most radical: in his utopia criminals are punished with the severest slavery.

Egotism and crime are the negative consequences of human freedom. When human beings developed the impulse of a free consciousness they had to leave Paradise. Freedom, the highest good of humanity, is at the same time a mortal sting for a harmonious society. The problem of utopia is the problem of freedom.

When we now take a look at Act 2 of *The Tempest*, we recognize this problem there. Gonzalo sketches his utopian island. The villainous mockers point to the weakness in his discourse: The ideal society is only possible if there is a king or ruler who *forces* happiness on the people.

Then follows the traitorous plot of the same two people to kill King Alonso in his sleep and thus seize the throne. In the dialogue leading up to this Sebastian poses the question to Antonio: "But for your conscience..." Antonio replies:

> Ay, sir; where lies that? If 't were a kybe,
> 'T would put me to my slipper; but I feel not
> This deity in my bosom; twenty consciences,
> That stand 'twixt me and Milan, candied be they
> And melt, ere they molest! [2.1]

No outside power, no matter how moral, is able to overcome the human being's treasonous egotism. It may be suppressed or controlled, but never cured. *That is only possible by means of conscience.*

In this regard, Shakespeare's utopia, the island of Prospero, is a refutation of More's *Utopia*. Shakespeare knew that the sanctification of the social order is only possible by the inner perfection of the human being. His utopia lies in the human soul or, in different words, his utopian island is an image of the soul world. Conscience is not in conflict with freedom. When we listen to the voice of our conscience, we do not act under compulsion but out of insight. Not fear of punishment but love of the good is the motivation of the human being who acts out of conscience.

Immediately after the failed attempt on the lives of Alonso and Gonzalo follows the scene in which Caliban enters into his ill-conceived alliance with Stefano and Trinculo. Suppressed evil and enforced servility rebel against the compelling strength of the good. Because this scene is so funny, we hardly notice that the poet points us to the heart of the social problem. The drunken Caliban dances and roars: " Freedom, high-day! high-day, freedom!"

Notice the sharp and heart-rending quality with which Shakespeare sketches this caricature of the freedom experience. How often do we not recognize the voice of the drunken Caliban in the freedom cries that impel people to violence and crime?

The second act has a perfectly grandiose structure: Gonzalo sketches his utopia in which everyone is free, but he tacitly sets himself up as king to see to it that freedom can only be used to the good and not for evil. In other words, evil as a consequence of freedom must be eliminated by authority. But that authority may then *never sleep*; it must be ever watchful. And then follows immediately the reality of evil which *never sleeps*: the murder plot.

At the same time an inner light dawns in Sebastian: he speaks of conscience. Antonio puts it out right away. The voice of conscience is the voice of the divine in the soul, the moral guiding star that has to replace moral authority and authoritarian law. When this voice is suppressed the monster in the soul is let loose. It stands up out of its oppression, chooses a drunken brute for its god, and fancies this new master to be its savior, the bringer of freedom.

It is hardly conceivable to represent the problem of state and society more concisely and brilliantly.

Shakespeare's Nova Atlantis

The utopian story that is the most important for our time had not yet been written during Shakespeare's life. It is Francis Bacon's story about New Atlantis, the manuscript of which remained unfinished and dates to 1624, eight years after Shakespeare's death.

Why is Bacon's *Nova Atlantis* so important for our time? Because it gives a picture of a society that is completely ruled by natural science. In this regard, Bacon's story is no utopia in the usual sense of the word. It is an ideal, and therefore unrealistic state; but it is also an extraordinarily real prophecy that has been fulfilled in our time.

Bacon describes his New Atlantis as an island, Bensalem, with a well-ordered society that is ruled by rational knowledge. This knowledge is collected, protected, and elaborated by the "House of Solomon," a brotherhood of scholars and technicians which, by its perfectly organized teamwork, is the most powerful institution in the world. According to one of these scholars the mission of the House of Solomon is: "Knowledge of the causes and movements of nature, as well as its hidden forces, and the extension of human rulership over these to the uttermost limits."

When we then read the description of all the things these New Atlanteans have and are capable of in their sub-earthly cooling centers, laboratories, factories, and observation towers, we are astonished to see that virtually all of this fantasy has today actually been realized. It reads like a story by Jules Verne whose fantasies, by the way, have also come true. One thing, however, is perfectly clear, namely that this gigantic scientific institute of Nova Atlantis works exclusively with those forces in nature that can be discovered by the human intellect through external observation.

Keeping our own civilization in mind, it is also most significant that the "House of Solomon" has the intention to artificially imitate the gifts of living nature including, for instance, meteorological phenomena. The scientific complex of the "House" is actually one huge factory of surrogates.

What will also strike us is the attitude of the New Atlanteans toward the rest of the world. Strangers are kept away from the island. Commercial relationships and cultural exchanges with other peoples do not exist. There is complete economic self-sufficiency and perfect state egotism. But every twelve years they do send scientific spies into the world who inconspicuously mix with people in other countries to collect everything they consider interesting: books, instruments, inventions, reports on political and social arrangements, et cetera; in brief, a kind of super press service combined with scientific espionage.

Although Bacon's tale exudes an atmosphere of humanness, idealism, religiosity, and optimism, we should not have any illusions as to the true character of this prophecy: we see here the most radical inversion of the impulses of Christian Rosenkreutz one can imagine (see the study of *As You Like It*). The traits of Rosicrucianism are evident: the brothers who go out into the world as unknown entities; a spiritual union of men who want to study the secrets of nature; and social arrangements that are the fruit of the wisdom of the brothers and improve the world.

But consider the contrast of Bacon's conception of this striving. The obscure and hidden character of the Solomon envoys guarantees their success as spies. The secrets of nature are only investigated in a materialistic sense, and social arrangements are not oriented toward the good of mankind but toward the "splendid isolation" of Nova Atlantis. It is stated with emphasis that the happy isle of Bensalem has nothing to do with supernatural forces. Everything that penetrates there as news of the world is not revealed by "air spirits" (!) that were sent out, but by the House of Solomon, the "eye" of the island, by purely natural means therefore.

Only the way in which Christianity reached the people of Nova Atlantis can indeed be called a miracle. Shortly after Christ, the books of the Old and New Testaments came to the island with the help of the apostle Bartholomew. The description of the arrival of the holy books in a little wooden chest in the sea, divinely indicated by a column of light and a cross, is a purely magical wonder and therefore as un-Christian as one can imagine. The event is rather like the miracles that are described in the tales of the Thousand and One Nights. One is also reminded of the revelation of the golden tablets of the Mormons.

Shakespeare did not know Bacon's story, but he had a presentiment of certain tendencies of his time. That Bacon would have seen *The Tempest* is not impossible, even quite probable. At any rate, there is a surprising relationship between these two brilliant, but contrasting, creations.

Prospero, the wise man of the tempest island, controls the forces of nature by means of magic. His occult development has enabled him to put the spiritual beings that work in natural phenomena in his service. His destiny moments and those of his servant, the air spirit Ariel, follow the Jupiter rhythm of twelve years. The wise men of the House of Solomon collect their information of the world in a rhythm of twelve years. Here, however, it is not about a framework of destiny, but about a purely outer process of collecting knowledge that will make rational control of the nature forces possible.

Christianity, for the New Atlanteans, is an external affair that came to them through a miraculous event. The frivolous manner in which Bacon weaves the Pentecost mystery into his report of the arrival of the holy books indicates clearly that for the author himself Christianity is similarly something that comes to him from the outside. For he relates that the Hebrew, Persians, and Indians who at that time still lived on the island could read the texts of the Christian books as if these had been written in their mother tongues. The true significance of the Holy Spirit at Pentecost, which enabled the apostles to speak the languages of all peoples in the sense of a "mission to humanity," must have completely passed Bacon by.

Nowhere in *The Tempest* does Shakespeare speak of Christianity, but he shows the inner reality of the Christ mystery in the dramatic development of his play. When Prospero has found Christian love, through which he can love his enemies and forgive those who treated him badly, he abjures his magic. He wants to live as a human being among human beings, using his wisdom to serve humanity, instead of building a kind of power center on his island. In his moving epilogue he asks the public, meaning all human beings, to help him leave his island by giving him their approval. He asks for the love of his fellow human beings, and he asks for mercy, divine love.

William Shakespeare, the pupil of Christian Rosenkreutz, who did not twist the inspirations of his Master in a materialistic sense, gave with his *Tempest* an answer to More's *Utopia*. He did so by reducing the problem of freedom and evil, in an inner sense, to the question of conscience. His prophetic answer to Bacon's

Nova Atlantis, which had not yet been written in 1611, is just as impressive: The moral question of human society is not solved by knowledge of nature, nor by magic in nature. It is only solved by christening the soul.

In ancient Atlantis, tens of thousands of years before Christ, the human being was still so intimately interwoven with natural events that natural law and moral law coincided. Magic was common. The Greeks preserved in their mythology and profound mystery wisdom a memory of these old Atlantean times. In that sense, Prospero is still an old Atlantean. He uses the nature being Ariel to awaken the morality of his enemies. He shows Ferdinand and Miranda the Greek goddesses of nature morality: Ceres (Demeter) and Juno (Hera).

But the turn to his new Atlantis is the change to the inner world. Moral power must now be found in the innermost part of the soul. When it is found, a new relationship to nature comes into being: Ariel is freed. Then "Atlantis" is no longer Atlantis, no island far from human civilization. Shakespeare's Atlantis expands to include the entire globe of earth.

Will humanity progress in the footprints of Francis Bacon, or take the trail indicated by Shakespeare? So far, Bacon has the upper hand. Shakespeare has more admirers, but Bacon more practitioners. Both figures are viewed in such a close relationship to each other that there are still many people who ascribe Shakespeare's dramatic works to Francis Bacon. That is one of the revilements the true Rosicrucians are exposed to.

Bacon is the inaugurator of empirical natural science, the father of materialism and the inventor of the motto, "Knowledge is power." His shadow falls on our current culture, although this shadow disguises itself as light. People work in his spirit when, out of their intellectual knowledge and technological power, they want to dominate the world from their "island of consciousness." In the name of humanity and progress, nature forces are misused and humanity is fettered to the material world. The social evils that are the consequences of Bacon's impulse are the animalization of the body, denial of the spirit, and suffocation of the soul. Although this impulse originated in the West, it now also dominates the peoples and races of the East, to the extent that they have been infected by materialism.

But in our culture there are also living expectations of a true light. The soul wants to rise up and meet the spirit. It wants to leave its island of consciousness, to be a human soul with its own "faint strength." Perhaps it also wants to listen to the inner God who speaks with the voice of a free conscience, after it has freed itself from outworn and ill-fitting Church dogmas and traditions that are only reminders of an older, expired bond with the spirit.

And if the soul indeed does want this; wants to be cured of the slavish enemy in itself, and of the compulsion and surrogate-nature of the respectable scholars of the "House of Solomon," it will be able to find itself, with its expectations, weaknesses, and trials; with its striving for catharsis and love, in the images of Shakespeare's works.

9 781621 481416